YOUR CHINESE
HOROSCOPE 1997

———◆———

ABOUT THE AUTHOR

Neil Somerville is one of the leading writers in the West on Chinese horoscopes. He has been interested in Eastern forms of divination for many years and believes that much can be learned from the ancient wisdom of the East. His annual book on Chinese horoscopes has built up an international following and *Your Chinese Horoscope 1997* marks the tenth year of publication. He is also the author of *Chinese Love Signs* (Thorsons, 1995).

Neil Somerville was born in the year of the Water Snake. His wife was born under the sign of the Monkey, his son is an Ox and daughter a Horse.

YOUR CHINESE HOROSCOPE 1997

NEIL SOMERVILLE

What the Year of the Ox holds in store for you

Thorsons
An Imprint of HarperCollinsPublishers

TO ROS, RICHARD AND EMILY

Thorsons
An Imprint of HarperCollins*Publishers*
77–85 Fulham Palace Road
Hammersmith, London W6 8JB
1160 Battery Street
San Francisco, California 94111–1213

Published by Thorsons 1996

10 9 8 7 6 5 4 3 2 1

© Neil Somerville 1996

Neil Somerville asserts the moral right to
be identified as the author of this work

A catalogue record for this book
is available from the British Library

ISBN 0 7225 3303 9

Printed in Great Britain by
Caledonian International Book Manufacturing Ltd,
Glasgow, G64

CONTENTS

————◆————

ACKNOWLEDGEMENTS

———◆◆———

In writing *Your Chinese Horoscope 1997* I am grateful for the assistance and support that those around me have given. I wish to acknowledge Theodora Lau's *The Handbook of Chinese Horoscopes* (Harper & Row, 1979; Arrow, 1981), which was particularly useful to me in my research.

In addition to Ms Lau's work, I commend the following books to those who wish to find out more about Chinese horoscopes: Kristyna Arcarti, *Chinese Horoscopes for Beginners* (Headway, 1995); Catherine Aubier, *Chinese Zodiac Signs* (Arrow, 1984), series of 12 books; Paula Delsol, *Chinese Horoscopes* (Pan, 1973); E. A. Crawford and Teresa Kennedy, *Chinese Elemental Astrology* (Piatkus, 1992); Barry Fantoni, *Barry Fantoni's Chinese Horoscopes* (Warner, 1994); Jean-Michel Huon de Kermadec, *The Way to Chinese Astrology* (Unwin, 1983); Kwok Man-Ho, *Authentic Chinese Horoscopes* (Arrow, 1987), series of 12 books; Paul Rigby and Harvey Bean, *Chinese Astrologics* (Publications Division, South China Morning Post Ltd., 1981), Derek Walters, *Ming Shu* (Pagoda Books, 1987) and *The Chinese Astrology Workbook* (The Aquarian Press, 1988), Suzanne White, *Suzanne White Book of Chinese Chance* (Fontana/Collins, 1978) and *The New Astrology* (Pan, 1987) and *The New Chinese Astrology* (Pan, 1994).

INTRODUCTION

The origins of Chinese horoscopes have been lost in the mists of time. It is known that oriental astrologers practised their art many thousands of years ago and, even today, Chinese astrology continues to fascinate and intrigue.

In Chinese astrology there are 12 signs named after 12 different animals. No one quite knows how the signs acquired their names, but there is one legend that offers an explanation.

According to this legend, one Chinese New Year, the Buddha invited all the animals in his kingdom to come before him. Unfortunately – for reasons best known to the animals – only 12 turned up. The first to arrive was the Rat, followed by the Ox, Tiger, Rabbit, Dragon, Snake, Horse, Goat, Monkey, Rooster, Dog and finally the Pig.

In gratitude, the Buddha decided to name a year after each of the animals and those born during that year would inherit some of the personality of that animal. Therefore those born in the year of the Ox would be hard-working, resolute and stubborn – just like the Ox – while those born in the year of the Dog would be loyal and faithful – just like the Dog.

While not everyone can possibly share all the characteristics of a sign, it is incredible what similarities do occur and this is partly where the fascination of Chinese horoscopes lies.

In addition to the 12 signs of the Chinese zodiac there are also five elements and these have a strengthening or moderating influence upon the sign. Details about the effects of the elements are given in each of the chapters on the 12 signs.

To find out which sign you were born under, refer to the tables on pages ix–xii. As the Chinese year is based on the lunar year and does not start until late January or early February, it is particularly important for anyone born in those two months to check carefully the dates of the Chinese year in which they were born.

Also included, in the Appendix, are two charts showing the compatibility between the signs for both personal and business relationships, and details about the signs ruling the different hours of the day. From this it is possible to locate your ascendant and, as in Western astrology, this has a significant influence on your personality.

In writing this book, I have taken the unusual step of combining the intriguing nature of Chinese horoscopes with the Western desire to know what the future holds and have based my interpretations upon various factors relating to each of the signs. This is the tenth year in which *Your Chinese Horoscope* has been published and I am pleased that so many have found the sections on the forth-coming year of benefit and that the advice has been constructive and helpful. Remember, though, that at all times you are the master of your own destiny. I sincerely hope that *Your Chinese Horoscope 1997* will prove inter-esting and helpful for the year ahead.

THE CHINESE YEARS

—◆—

Rat	31 January	1900	to	18 February	1901
Ox	19 February	1901	to	7 February	1902
Tiger	8 February	1902	to	28 January	1903
Rabbit	29 January	1903	to	15 February	1904
Dragon	16 February	1904	to	3 February	1905
Snake	4 February	1905	to	24 January	1906
Horse	25 January	1906	to	12 February	1907
Goat	13 February	1907	to	1 February	1908
Monkey	2 February	1908	to	21 January	1909
Rooster	22 January	1909	to	9 February	1910
Dog	10 February	1910	to	29 January	1911
Pig	30 January	1911	to	17 February	1912
Rat	18 February	1912	to	5 February	1913
Ox	6 February	1913	to	25 January	1914
Tiger	26 January	1914	to	13 February	1915
Rabbit	14 February	1915	to	2 February	1916
Dragon	3 February	1916	to	22 January	1917
Snake	23 January	1917	to	10 February	1918
Horse	11 February	1918	to	31 January	1919
Goat	1 February	1919	to	19 February	1920
Monkey	20 February	1920	to	7 February	1921
Rooster	8 February	1921	to	27 January	1922
Dog	28 January	1922	to	15 February	1923
Pig	16 February	1923	to	4 February	1924

Rat	5 February	1924	to	23 January	1925
Ox	24 January	1925	to	12 February	1926
Tiger	13 February	1926	to	1 February	1927
Rabbit	2 February	1927	to	22 January	1928
Dragon	23 January	1928	to	9 February	1929
Snake	10 February	1929	to	29 January	1930
Horse	30 January	1930	to	16 February	1931
Goat	17 February	1931	to	5 February	1932
Monkey	6 February	1932	to	25 January	1933
Rooster	26 January	1933	to	13 February	1934
Dog	14 February	1934	to	3 February	1935
Pig	4 February	1935	to	23 January	1936
Rat	24 January	1936	to	10 February	1937
Ox	11 February	1937	to	30 January	1938
Tiger	31 January	1938	to	18 February	1939
Rabbit	19 February	1939	to	7 February	1940
Dragon	8 February	1940	to	26 January	1941
Snake	27 January	1941	to	14 February	1942
Horse	15 February	1942	to	4 February	1943
Goat	5 February	1943	to	24 January	1944
Monkey	25 January	1944	to	12 February	1945
Rooster	13 February	1945	to	1 February	1946
Dog	2 February	1946	to	21 January	1947
Pig	22 January	1947	to	9 February	1948
Rat	10 February	1948	to	28 January	1949
Ox	29 January	1949	to	16 February	1950
Tiger	17 February	1950	to	5 February	1951
Rabbit	6 February	1951	to	26 January	1952
Dragon	27 January	1952	to	13 February	1953
Snake	14 February	1953	to	2 February	1954
Horse	3 February	1954	to	23 January	1955

Goat	24 January	1955	to	11 February	1956
Monkey	12 February	1956	to	30 January	1957
Rooster	31 January	1957	to	17 February	1958
Dog	18 February	1958	to	7 February	1959
Pig	8 February	1959	to	27 January	1960
Rat	28 January	1960	to	14 February	1961
Ox	15 February	1961	to	4 February	1962
Tiger	5 February	1962	to	24 January	1963
Rabbit	25 January	1963	to	12 February	1964
Dragon	13 February	1964	to	1 February	1965
Snake	2 February	1965	to	20 January	1966
Horse	21 January	1966	to	8 February	1967
Goat	9 February	1967	to	29 January	1968
Monkey	30 January	1968	to	16 February	1969
Rooster	17 February	1969	to	5 February	1970
Dog	6 February	1970	to	26 January	1971
Pig	27 January	1971	to	14 February	1972
Rat	15 February	1972	to	2 February	1973
Ox	3 February	1973	to	22 January	1974
Tiger	23 January	1974	to	10 February	1975
Rabbit	11 February	1975	to	30 January	1976
Dragon	31 January	1976	to	17 February	1977
Snake	18 February	1977	to	6 February	1978
Horse	7 February	1978	to	27 January	1979
Goat	28 January	1979	to	15 February	1980
Monkey	16 February	1980	to	4 February	1981
Rooster	5 February	1981	to	24 January	1982
Dog	25 January	1982	to	12 February	1983
Pig	13 February	1983	to	1 February	1984
Rat	2 February	1984	to	19 February	1985
Ox	20 February	1985	to	8 February	1986

Tiger	9 February	1986	to	28 January	1987
Rabbit	29 January	1987	to	16 February	1988
Dragon	17 February	1988	to	5 February	1989
Snake	6 February	1989	to	26 January	1990
Horse	27 January	1990	to	14 February	1991
Goat	15 February	1991	to	3 February	1992
Monkey	4 February	1992	to	22 January	1993
Rooster	23 January	1993	to	9 February	1994
Dog	10 February	1994	to	30 January	1995
Pig	31 January	1995	to	18 February	1996
Rat	19 February	1996	to	6 February	1997
Ox	7 February	1997	to	27 January	1998

Note: The names of the signs in the Chinese zodiac occasionally differ in the various books on Chinese astrology, although the characteristics of the signs remain the same. In some books the Ox is referred to as the Buffalo or Bull, the Rabbit as the Hare or Cat, the Goat as the Sheep and the Pig as the Boar.

For the sake of convenience, the male gender is used throughout this book. Unless otherwise stated, the characteristics of the signs apply to both sexes.

The Ox year favours the industrious and those who are prepared to make the effort. What you put into the year, you will get out. Sow much, reap much; sow little, reap little.

Chinese proverb

WELCOME TO
THE YEAR OF THE OX

Whether ploughing fields or carrying heavy loads, the Ox has served mankind well for thousands of years. Strong, hard-working and reliable, the Ox is a dutiful worker. This sense of duty, of commitment and hard work will be evident in the Ox's own year. Much can and will be achieved in 1997; it will not necessarily be an easy year, but it will herald some important changes and significant events.

Throughout the year there will be a feeling that action brings results and, in almost all spheres of life, positive steps will be taken to bring about change and improvement. The Ox year is certainly not a year for malaise or a soft-hearted 'wait and see' approach, but a year for committed and determined action.

On the world stage there will be several major summits which will result in a closer spirit of co-operation between nations, stimulate world trade and also deal with some of the world's more vexing problems. It was an Ox year when Nixon and Brezhnev signed a historic arms limitation agreement and in the last Ox year Reagan met the new Soviet leader Gorbachev, a meeting which marked the beginning of improved relations between the superpowers. This pattern will continue in 1997 and some of the meetings that take place will have far-reaching consequences. In previous Ox years NATO came into force and the Council of Europe was established, and 1997 is not only likely to see a widening of the Common Market but also important developments within NATO.

Previous Ox years have also seen significant changes in the leadership of many countries and 1997 will be no exception. Almost certainly new and powerful figures will emerge on the world stage and some will have a major impact in the years leading up to the twenty-first century.

The Ox year could also see several governments and leaders coming under close scrutiny for their policies and past actions. In some cases, this will lead to weeks of speculation, uncertainty and even the resignation of some leading figures. It was in the Ox year of 1973 that the Watergate scandal gathered momentum and in the next one of 1985 that the Westland affair rocked the Thatcher administration; some events in 1997 will bring about some uncomfortable moments for present governments.

As far as domestic policy is concerned, there will be considerable emphasis on law and order and steps will be taken in many countries to curb the escalation in crime. This will not only include the introduction of stiffer penalties for certain offences but also greater vigilance. There will be closer co-operation between countries to combat international crime. Similarly, challenges to the rule of law will be severely dealt with and in 1997 few governments will countenance the demands of illegally held strikes, protests or terrorists. In the Ox year, law and order reign supreme and while there will be challenges to the Ox's authority, rarely will these succeed.

There will also be considerable emphasis on education

YOUR CHINESE HOROSCOPE 1997

and training over the year and many governments will provide large amounts of additional funding for education as well as encourage many to undertake further training. Those seeking work will be urged to learn new skills and some major new training initiatives will be introduced. Large companies will also be encouraged to make more work experience places and job training opportunities available and those who are able to take advantage of these could find them of long-term benefit.

The Ox year will also see some major technological advances. Man was first launched into space in an Ox year, the first jet engine was built and on a domestic level, Clarence Birdseye invented the frozen food process which was to revolutionize modern day catering. In 1997 this pattern of achievement will continue. It is also likely that several major companies will pool their resources and merge over the year, the consequences of which will be profound for certain industries – especially in the telecommunication, media and pharmaceutical fields. In addition, there will be significant advances in global communication and systems such as the Internet will become even more widespread. Indeed, what will be achieved in this, the last Ox year of the century, will seem a long way removed to the first Ox year when, in 1901, Marconi succeeded in sending the first transmitted signal across the Atlantic!

There will, however, be concern in 1997 over changes to the world's climate and several continents will experience changed weather patterns which could, in some cases, result in suffering and hardship.

More positively, however, the growth that has been seen in the economies of many countries over recent years will continue at a steady, if not rapid, pace. This will be reflected in the generally optimistic nature of stock markets around the world, although there could be several large movements in prices – both up and down! – with the result that investors will need to remain vigilant throughout the year.

Another feature of the year will be a noticeable emphasis on health and fitness. Many will feel motivated to take better care of themselves and, in addition to improvements in diet and the increasing demand for pure and organic foods, there will be a significant growth in the number of those engaging in active leisure pursuits such as gardening, rambling, swimming, cycling or physical fitness courses.

The Ox also has an affinity for the land and there will be a continuing appreciation of the value of the countryside. Damage to the environment or attempts to encroach upon areas of natural beauty for building purposes are likely to result in widespread condemnation. Environmental pressure groups could be particularly active in 1997, sometimes coming into direct conflict with those in authority.

For most, however, 1997 will be a positive year and the Ox year will reward those who are prepared to work hard and make the effort. While some signs will fare better than others, almost all can make progress and gain something of value from the year. It is, however, those with commitment and drive who succeed in the Ox year and, as Henry David Thoreau, himself an Ox, once wrote, 'I know of no more encouraging fact than the unquestionable ability of man to elevate his life by a conscious endeavour.'

In 1997 many will feel inspired to make that conscious endeavour and will reap the benefit as a result.

---

31 JANUARY 1900 ∿ 18 FEBRUARY 1901	*Metal Rat*
18 FEBRUARY 1912 ∿ 5 FEBRUARY 1913	*Water Rat*
5 FEBRUARY 1924 ∿ 23 JANUARY 1925	*Wood Rat*
24 JANUARY 1936 ∿ 10 FEBRUARY 1937	*Fire Rat*
10 FEBRUARY 1948 ∿ 28 JANUARY 1949	*Earth Rat*
28 JANUARY 1960 ∿ 14 FEBRUARY 1961	*Metal Rat*
15 FEBRUARY 1972 ∿ 2 FEBRUARY 1973	*Water Rat*
2 FEBRUARY 1984 ∿ 19 FEBRUARY 1985	*Wood Rat*
19 FEBRUARY 1996 ∿ 6 FEBRUARY 1997	*Fire Rat*

THE
RAT

THE PERSONALITY OF THE RAT

One man in his time plays many parts.
– William Shakespeare: a Rat

The Rat is born under the sign of charm. He is intelligent, popular and loves attending parties and large social gatherings. He is able to establish friendships with remarkable ease and people generally feel relaxed in his company. He is a very social creature and is genuinely interested in the welfare and activities of others. He has a good understanding of human nature and his advice and opinions are often sought.

The Rat is a hard and diligent worker. He is also very imaginative and is never short of ideas. However, he does sometimes lack the confidence to promote his ideas as much as he should and this can often prevent him from securing the recognition and credit he so often deserves.

The Rat is very observant and many Rats have made excellent writers and journalists. The Rat also excels at personnel and PR work and any job which brings him into contact with people and the media. His skills are particularly appreciated in times of crisis, for the Rat has an incredibly strong sense of self-preservation. When it comes to finding a way out of an awkward situation, he is certain to be the one who comes up with a solution.

The Rat loves to be where there is a lot of action, but should he ever find himself in a very bureaucratic or restrictive environment he can become a stickler for discipline and routine.

He is also something of an opportunist and is constantly on the look-out for ways in which he can improve his wealth and lifestyle. He rarely lets an opportunity go by and can become involved in so many plans and schemes that he sometimes squanders his energies and achieves very little as a result. He is also rather gullible and can be taken in by those less scrupulous than himself.

Another characteristic of the Rat is his attitude to money. He is very thrifty and to some he may appear a little mean. The reason for this is purely that he likes to keep his money within his family. He can be most generous to his partner, his children and close friends and relatives. He can also be generous to himself, for he often finds it impossible to deprive himself of any luxury or object he fancies. The Rat is also very acquisitive and can be a notorious hoarder. He hates waste and is rarely prepared to throw anything away. He can also be rather greedy and will rarely refuse an invitation for a free meal or a complimentary ticket to some lavish function.

The Rat is a good conversationalist, although he can occasionally be a little indiscreet. He can be highly critical of others – for an honest and unbiased opinion, the Rat is a superb critic – and sometimes will use confidential information to his own advantage. However, as the Rat has such a bright and irresistible nature, most are prepared to forgive him for his slight indiscretions.

Throughout his long and eventful life, the Rat will make many friends and will find that he is especially well-suited to those born under his own sign and those of the Ox, Dragon and Monkey. He can also get on well with those born under the signs of the Tiger, Snake, Rooster, Dog and

Pig, but the rather sensitive Rabbit and Goat will find the Rat a little too critical and blunt for their liking. The Horse and Rat will also find it difficult to get on with each other – the Rat craves security and will find the Horse's changeable moods and rather independent nature a little unsettling.

The Rat is very family orientated and will do anything to please his nearest and dearest. He is exceptionally loyal to his parents and can himself be a very caring and loving parent. He will take an interest in all his children's activities and will see that they want for nothing. The Rat usually has a large family.

The female Rat has a kindly, outgoing nature and involves herself in a multitude of different activities. She has a wide circle of friends, enjoys entertaining and is an attentive hostess. She is also conscientious about the upkeep of her home and has superb taste in home furnishings. She is most supportive to the other members of her family and, due to her resourceful, friendly and persevering nature, can do well in practically any career she enters.

Although the Rat is essentially outgoing and something of an extrovert, he is also a very private individual. He tends to keep his feelings to himself and, while he is not averse to learning what other people are doing, he resents anyone prying too closely into his own affairs. He also does not like solitude and if he is alone for any length of time he can easily get depressed.

The Rat is undoubtedly very talented, but more often than not he fails to capitalize on his many abilities. He has a tendency to become involved in too many schemes and chase after too many opportunities all at one time. If he were to slow down and concentrate on one thing at a time he could become very successful. If not, success and wealth could elude him. But the Rat, with his tremendous ability to charm will rarely, if ever, be without friends.

THE FIVE DIFFERENT TYPES OF RAT

In addition to the 12 signs of the Chinese zodiac, there are five elements and these have a strengthening or moderating influence on the sign. The effects of the five elements on the Rat are described below, together with the years in which the elements were exercising their influence. Therefore all Rats born in 1900 and 1960 are Metal Rats, those born in 1912 and 1972 are Water Rats, and so on.

Metal Rat: 1900, 1960
This Rat has excellent taste and certainly knows how to appreciate the finer things in life. His home is comfortable and nicely decorated and he is forever entertaining or mixing in fashionable circles. He has considerable financial acumen and invests his money well. On the surface the Metal Rat appears cheerful and confident, but deep down he can be troubled by worries that are quite often of his own making. He is exceptionally loyal to his family and friends.

Water Rat: 1912, 1972

The Water Rat is intelligent and very astute. He is a deep thinker and can express his thoughts clearly and persuasively. He is always eager to learn and is talented in many different areas. The Water Rat is usually very popular, but his fear of loneliness can sometimes lead him into mixing with the wrong sort of company. He is a particularly skilful writer, but he can get side-tracked very easily and should try to concentrate on just one thing at a time.

Wood Rat: 1924, 1984

The Wood Rat has a friendly, outgoing personality and is most popular with his colleagues and friends. He has a quick, agile brain and likes to turn his hand to anything he thinks may be useful. His one fear is insecurity, but given his intelligence and capabilities, this fear is usually unfounded. He has a good sense of humour, enjoys travel and, due to his highly imaginative nature, can be a gifted writer or artist.

Fire Rat: 1936, 1996

The Fire Rat is rarely still and seems to have a never-ending supply of energy and enthusiasm. He loves being involved in the action – be it travel, following up new ideas or campaigning for a cause in which he fervently believes. He is an original thinker and hates being bound by petty restrictions or the dictates of others. He can be forthright in his views, but can sometimes get carried away in the excitement of the moment and commit himself to various undertakings without checking what all the implications might be. He has a resilient nature and, with the right support, can often go far in life.

Earth Rat: 1948

This Rat is astute and very level-headed. He rarely takes unnecessary chances and, while he is constantly trying to improve his financial status, he is prepared to proceed slowly and leave nothing to chance. The Earth Rat is probably not as adventurous as the other types of Rat and prefers to remain in familiar areas rather than rush headlong into something he knows little about. He is talented, conscientious and caring towards his loved ones, but at the same time can be self-conscious and worry a little too much about the image he is trying to project.

PROSPECTS FOR THE RAT IN 1997

The Chinese New Year starts on 7 February 1997. Until then, the old year, the Year of the Rat, is still making its presence felt.

The Year of the Rat (19 February 1996 to 6 February 1997) is the Rat's own year and is a most positive time for him. During the year he can make progress in almost all areas of his life and, provided he remains committed to his objectives, can achieve much. This is especially so in the last few months of the year.

In his work, the Rat can make particularly good progress and should actively follow up any openings or opportunities he sees. He should also promote any ideas he has; he will find them favourably received and they will do much to further his prospects. Those Rats who are dissatisfied with their current situation would do well to keep alert for opportunities, with September and October 1995 being active months for employment matters.

Financially, the Rat year is also a favoured time. However, while the Rat will do well in money matters, it would still be in his interests to remain his thrifty self. To be overly indulgent or splash out on too many whims could quickly deplete his savings. If possible, he should consider setting a regular amount to one side for a specific purpose or saving it for the holiday period at the end of the year. If he does, he could be pleasantly surprised with just how much he is able to accumulate in this way.

Both socially and domestically the closing stages of the Rat year will be an enjoyable time and the Rat will find himself much in demand with those around him. He can also look forward to attending some enjoyable social functions in the closing weeks of the year and these will help him to add to his already large number of friends and acquaintances. For those seeking romance, November and December could prove two most auspicious months. As far as personal relations are concerned, the Rat will be on top form and should he have any worries, uncertainties or problems in the latter part of the year, he should not hesitate to seek the advice and assistance of others. This, he will find will be readily forthcoming.

Generally the Rat year treats the Rat well and in what remains of it, he should take advantage of the favourable trends and opportunities. For the bold and enterprising Rat, much can be achieved in the closing months of the year.

The Year of the Ox begins on 7 February and will be a reasonable year for the Rat. Although he may not have things all his own way during the year, he will still be able to make a fair amount of progress as well as enjoy some pleasing times with those around him.

To get the best from the Ox year, however, the Rat would do well to take stock of his present position and decide upon his objectives for the next 12 months. Then, with some plans in mind, no matter what area of his life they might concern, he should work purposefully towards attaining those objectives. The one thing he should avoid in the Ox year is over-committing himself or trying to engage in too many activities all at the same time. Progress in 1997 will come from self-discipline, careful planning and applied effort. For the persistent and conscientious Rat, the rewards of the year can prove substantial.

In his work the Rat will continue to impress and there will be several opportunities for him to take on new and more remunerative duties or for him to move to a different position. The later months of the year are especially favourable for career matters, with late August to November being a significant time. However, while the Rat is often masterful at getting round others or using his persuasive abilities to get his own way, this may not be enough in 1997. In the Ox year the Rat will need to work hard and persevere in his activities.

The Rat is also adept at spotting opportunities and during the year he will indeed see several tempting ones. However, he would do well to investigate these more fully before committing himself to any new undertaking. All may not be as straightforward as it might appear and the Rat should be wary of embarking on any major new venture without careful thought and preparation. In many ways, this year he will achieve more by sticking to familiar areas than by getting involved in activities in which he does not have so much knowledge or experience.

Should the Rat have any uncertainties or problems concerning his work, he should speak of his concerns to others, particularly to those who have experience or are in a position to help. Although the Rat does like to remain his own master, he will find any worries that he does have will be considerably eased by discussing them openly rather than keeping them to himself. The Rat is indeed in the fortunate position of having many he can turn to for advice and in 1997 he should not hesitate to avail himself of this support.

The Rat will also need to exercise a certain care when dealing with monetary matters. The Ox year is not a year when he can either be complacent or take risks with his finances. If he has any uncertainties over any transaction he is about to enter into, he would be wise to check the details carefully and make sure he is aware of any obligations he may be placed under. Also, if there is an expensive item he desires, he would do well to investigate the prices in several places rather than buy it straightaway. This way he could save himself a considerable amount of money. Provided the Rat is careful in the way he handles his money he should avoid running into problems, but this is not a year when he can trust his luck too far.

The Rat's domestic life will, however, give him considerable pleasure and he can look forward to some memorable

THE RAT

times with those close to him. In particular, he will take much delight in following the successes and progress enjoyed by someone younger than himself and any assistance he feels able to give will be much appreciated. He would also do well to fully involve his family in his own activities and be prepared to discuss his views and ideas with them; he will be much encouraged by the advice and support he is given. However, while domestic matters will generally go well, he should not be overly demanding of others and expect all to fall in with his plans. The Rat may have very definite ideas on what he wants done but to expect others to agree with him all the time could result in disputes and moments of tension. Throughout the Ox year the Rat does need to remain mindful of others if he wishes to preserve domestic harmony.

The Rat's social life will also be pleasurable and he can look forward to attending some enjoyable events over the year. The summer months in particular will be a most auspicious time, especially for those seeking romance or wanting to make new friends. Any Rats who move in 1997 will also take much delight in building up a new social life and, with their personable manner, they will quickly impress and befriend others. The Rat will obtain much satisfaction from his various hobbies over the year and, while he may have many calls upon his time, he should still ensure that he sets a regular time aside for them. They do provide him with an important break from his usual daily activities, as well as being a valuable source of relaxation. Creative activities will go especially well and for the many Rats who enjoy writing, painting, music or some other aspect of the arts, it would certainly be in their interests to further their talents and promote their work for it is likely to be most favourably received. Also, those Rats who do not get much exercise during the day could find some additional activity such as walking, swimming or cycling beneficial for them.

The Rat will also enjoy the travelling that he undertakes over the year as well as take much delight in visiting local places of interest. He could find trips arranged at short notice especially pleasant.

Generally, the Rat will have good reason to enjoy 1997. Much will go in his favour and, in addition to having some pleasing times with his family and friends, almost all Rats will have the opportunity to improve upon their present position. However, in the Year of the Ox, the Rat does need to remain committed to his objectives and be prepared to work hard. Progress is certainly possible but it does require effort on his part.

As far as the different types of Rat are concerned, 1997 will be both a constructive and pleasant year for the *Metal Rat*. Although his progress may not always be smooth, his efforts and diligence will be much appreciated and during the year he will do much to improve upon his present position. Admittedly there may be times when he may feel disenchanted with what he is doing or feel that he is not making the progress that he would like, but he should not allow this to weaken his resolve. All the time he will be winning the support and respect of others and later in the year he will find his efforts recognized and rewarded. Some Metal Rats can look forward to promotion and being given more challenging responsibilities, while others will be successful in obtaining a better position elsewhere. Those Metal Rats seeking work or wanting a complete change of duties should remain alert for openings and also investigate different ways in which they can use their many talents. The Metal Rat has a most resourceful nature as well as possessing a good sense of opportunism and these traits will serve him well over the year. The second half of the Ox year will prove particularly significant for employment matters, with October and November being important months. The Metal Rat will also fare reasonably well in financial matters, although he would still do well to keep a careful watch over his general level of expenditure. He could find it helpful to review his outgoings regularly and cut back on any expenses no longer necessary or essential; this way the Metal Rat could make some savings which would allow him to put his money to more effective use. Domestically the year will go well for him and he will have every reason to be proud of the successes enjoyed by those around him. Any further assistance and encouragement he feels able to give to family members will be greatly valued. However, throughout the year, the Metal Rat does need to remain aware of the feelings of those close to him and, should he meet with any resistance to his own ideas or plans, he should be prepared to discuss this rather than carry on regardless. To do so could give rise to ill-feeling and mar what will otherwise be a generally happy year. The Metal Rat's social life will also give him considerable pleasure and he can look forward to attending some memorable parties and functions over the summer months. Although he may not travel as far as he has done in recent years, he should still make sure that he takes a holiday or decent break over the year. Also, he should not neglect his hobbies and interests as these do provide a valuable source of relaxation for him. Generally this will be a pleasant year for the Metal Rat and, by setting about his activities in his usual careful and conscientious manner, he will be well pleased with his achievements. The second half of the year will go particularly well.

This will be an interesting year for the *Water Rat* and one in which he will gain much valuable experience. Admittedly he may not accomplish all that he would like over the year, but he should not despair. He has many fine abilities and is highly regarded by others, and some of the frustrations he may face could stem from what he is trying to achieve. Some Water Rats could be attempting things without the necessary experience or trying to achieve too much too soon. Time is very much on the Water Rat's side and providing he continues to set about his activities in his usual diligent manner, he will be continually adding to his experience and preparing the way for the significant advances he will make in the near future. In some respects the Water Rat should regard 1997 as a year for learning, for consolidating his position and for preparing himself for future advancement. In his work, and also for those seeking work, the Water Rat would do well to take advantage of any training courses for which he might be eligible and look at ways he can use and broaden his skills. What the Water Rat learns in 1997 will prove most important to him later in the Ox year and in future years as well. The Water Rat will enjoy a gradual improvement in his financial situation over the year and by remaining alert, particularly at sale times, he could acquire some items for himself and his home at most favourable prices. He would also do well to consider setting a regular sum aside for a holiday or some short breaks over the year; he will find a change of scene most beneficial for him. Financially, the year will go well but, as with all Rats, this is not a year for complacency or for taking financial risks. The Water Rat's domestic life will be busy and at times demanding, but it will also give him a great sense of pride and satisfaction. However, if at any time he feels too much is being asked of him, he should not hesitate to seek the assistance and advice of those around him. He will find support readily forth-coming. For the unattached Water Rat, 1997 will prove a memorable year and he can look forward to an active and enjoyable social life as well as having the opportunity to establish several new and valuable friendships. Any Water Rat who may be feeling lonely or who has had some recent adversity to contend with would do well to regard 1997 as the start of a new phase in his life and should aim to go out more and get in contact with others. As with most things in 1997, positive action on his part will bring pleasing results. Generally, the Water Rat will enjoy the Ox year and while he may not always accomplish as much as he would like, what he does achieve over the year will do much to lay the foundations for his future prosperity.

This may not be the easiest of years for the *Wood Rat* but it will still prove an important one. At times during the year he could find his level of progress slow and that some of the things asked of him are difficult to carry out. Indeed, some of 1997 will prove challenging and a little frustrating, but the Wood Rat should not get disheartened. Over the year he will gain much valuable experience and will also learn more by rising up to the challenges given him rather than finding things all too easy. This will be a year when the Wood Rat will need to work hard and give of his best but, in the long run, he will find his efforts well rewarded. However, when the Wood Rat does have any matters concerning him, he should seek the advice of others rather than keep his anxieties to himself. He will find those around him will be only too pleased to help and will do much to alleviate any concerns he may have. In 1997 he will find much truth in the saying 'A worry shared is a worry halved.' However, while 1997 will be a demanding year, there will also be much that the Wood Rat will enjoy. Socially this will be a happy and fulfilling year and he will find himself much in demand with his many good friends. The spring months in particular could be a busy time and for those Wood Rats seeking additional friends, this is the time when they should really make every effort to go out more and get in contact with others. The Wood Rat will also take much pride in the successes enjoyed by family members over the year and domestically this will be a generally settled and content year. The Wood Rat would, however, do well to take note of any advice he is given; those around him do have his best interests at heart and there will be much wisdom in what he is told. Any holidays and breaks he takes over the year will prove most enjoyable and if he gets the opportunity to visit a place he has wanted to see for some time, this would be an excellent year to do so. Although the year will bring its challenges, what the Wood Rat learns and accomplishes will hold him in excellent stead for the future.

This is a year that the *Fire Rat* will enjoy and he can

accomplish much, although in many of his activities he will need to impose a little self-discipline upon himself. For all his enterprise and enthusiasm, this is not a year when he can take too many risks or set about new undertakings without planning and much careful thought. If he does, problems and disappointments could result. Over the year the Fire Rat will need to proceed at a measured pace and make sure that he has backing and support for his various endeavours. Similarly, if he has any doubts or uncertainties about any activity in which he is engaged, he would do well to seek advice rather than pressing on regardless. This is a year for caution and for working in close co-operation with others. Those Fire Rats in work can make good progress over the year but, as with most things, this will come from planning and hard work rather than from taking undue risks. On a domestic level, the Fire Rat will be pleased with any projects that he carries out around his home, especially any redecorating he does, although he should take extra care when moving heavy objects or doing anything of a hazardous nature. A strain or minor accident could lead to considerable discomfort. The Fire Rat can, however, look forward to some enjoyable times with those around him as well as being actively involved in several important family and social occasions. From a personal point of view, this will be a happy and fulfilling year. The Fire Rat will also obtain considerable satisfaction from his various interests and if he can extend them in any way, either by attending a course, by further reading or by getting in contact with fellow enthusiasts, he will find this will make them all the more meaningful. Also, if he has a hobby of a creative nature he should bring his work to the attention of others. It will be favourably received and the Fire Rat could find an interest or skill he has will prove unexpectedly remunerative over the year. Generally, 1997 will be a pleasurable year for the Fire Rat but to get the best from the year he does need to plan his activities well and avoid taking unnecessary risks.

This is a year that will suit the *Earth Rat* and one in which he will make steady progress. Unlike some previous years, the Ox year is unlikely to bring with it sudden or dramatic change and this will allow the Earth Rat to build on his present position and make the changes he wants rather than have them inflicted upon him. Those Earth Rats in work will make substantial progress and many will find their conscientiousness and reliability rewarded with new and more remunerative duties. Earth Rats who wish to move to different duties or who are seeking employment will also find new openings to pursue and even if they find any new position they are given initially daunting it will, in time, become a position they will very much enjoy. Naturally no year will be without its challenges, but those that do occur will prove a valuable learning experience for the Earth Rat and in meeting them he will win the admiration of many as well as do much to enhance his reputation. The Earth Rat will also enjoy an improvement in his financial situation and while he will naturally enjoy this upturn, if he is able to set some money aside for a specific purpose, such as home improvements or holidays, he will be glad he has done so. The Earth Rat's domestic life is, however, likely to be busy over the year and there will be many matters that will require his attention. However, while there may be times when he will despair of all he has to do, his home life will bring him considerable pleasure and he will delight in the achievements of those around him. Many Earth Rats will also have good reason for a family celebration over the year and this could include a marriage in the family, the birth of a grandchild or another event which will cause considerable rejoicing. The Earth Rat will also derive much pleasure from his social life and for those seeking new friends or who are unattached, a new friendship they make in the summer will prove both significant and meaningful. The Earth Rat should also make sure that he sets a regular time aside for his hobbies and recreational interests, even though he may sometimes feel there are more pressing things he ought to do. His interests will prove both satisfying and beneficial for him, particularly as they provide an important break from his everyday concerns. Generally 1997 will be a pleasing year for the Earth Rat and providing he sets about his activities with care and in his usual conscientious manner, he will acquit himself well and enjoy the year.

FAMOUS RATS

Alan Alda, Dave Allen, Ursula Andress, Louis Armstrong, Charles Aznavour, Lauren Bacall, Shirley Bassey, Jeremy Beadle, Irving Berlin, Virginia Bottomley, Kenneth Branagh, Marlon Brando, Charlotte Brontë, Chris de Burgh, George Bush, Lord Callaghan, Glen Campbell, Jimmy Carter, Dick Cavett, Raymond Chandler, Maurice Chevalier, Linford Christie, Barbara Dickson, Benjamin Disraeli, Noël Edmonds, T. S. Eliot, Albert Finney, Clark

Gable, Al Gore, Hugh Grant, Thomas Hardy, Mata Hari, Vaclav Havel, Haydn, Charlton Heston, Damon Hill, Ian Hislop, Dennis Hopper, Mick Hucknall, Roy Hudd, Engelbert Humperdinck, Jeremy Irons, Glenda Jackson, Jean-Michel Jarre, Gene Kelly, F. W. de Klerk, Kris Kristofferson, Lawrence of Arabia, Gary Lineker, Sir Andrew Lloyd Webber, Lulu, Claude Monet, Earl Mountbatten, Robert Mugabe, Richard Nixon, Robert Palmer, Sean Penn, Terry Pratchett, the Queen Mother, Vanessa Redgrave, Burt Reynolds, Jonathan Ross, Rossini, Emma Samms, William Shakespeare, Yves St Laurent, Tommy Steele, Donna Summer, James Taylor, Leo Tolstoy, Spencer Tracey, Anthea Turner, the Prince of Wales, George Washington, Dennis Waterman, Dennis Weaver, Roger Whittaker, Richard Wilson, Bill Wyman, the Duke of York, Emile Zola.

19 FEBRUARY 1901 ～ 7 FEBRUARY 1902   *Metal Ox*

6 FEBRUARY 1913 ～ 25 JANUARY 1914   *Water Ox*

24 JANUARY 1925 ～ 12 FEBRUARY 1926   *Wood Ox*

11 FEBRUARY 1937 ～ 30 JANUARY 1938   *Fire Ox*

29 JANUARY 1949 ～ 16 FEBRUARY 1950   *Earth Ox*

15 FEBRUARY 1961 ～ 4 FEBRUARY 1962   *Metal Ox*

3 FEBRUARY 1973 ～ 22 JANUARY 1974   *Water Ox*

20 FEBRUARY 1985 ～ 8 FEBRUARY 1986   *Wood Ox*

7 FEBRUARY 1997 ～ 27 JANUARY 1998   *Fire Ox*

THE
OX

THE PERSONALITY OF THE OX

Victory belongs to the most persevering.
> – *Napoleon Bonaparte: an Ox*

The Ox is born under the signs of equilibrium and tenacity. He is a hard and conscientious worker and sets about everything he does in a resolute, methodical and determined manner. He has considerable leadership qualities and is often admired for his tough and uncompromising nature. He knows what he wants to achieve in life and, as far as possible, will not be deflected from his ultimate objective.

The Ox takes his responsibilities and duties very seriously. He is decisive and quick to take advantage of any opportunity that comes his way. He is also sincere and places a great deal of trust in his friends and colleagues. He is, nevertheless, something of a loner. He is a quiet and private individual and often keeps his thoughts to himself. He also cherishes his independence and prefers to set about things in his own way rather than be bound by the dictates of others or be influenced by outside pressures.

The Ox tends to have a calm and tranquil nature, but if something angers him or he feels that someone has let him down, he can have a fearsome temper. He can also be stubborn and obstinate and this can lead him into conflict with others. Usually the Ox will succeed in getting his own way, but should things go against him, he is a poor loser and will take any defeat or set-back extremely badly.

The Ox is often a deep thinker and rather studious. He is

not particularly renowned for his sense of humour and does not take kindly to new gimmicks or anything too innovative. The Ox is too solid and traditional for that and he prefers to stick to the more conventional norm.

His home is very important to him and in some respects he treats it as a private sanctuary. His family tends to be closely knit and the Ox will make sure that each member does their fair share around the house. The Ox tends to be a hoarder, but he is always well-organized and neat. He also places great importance on punctuality and there is nothing that infuriates him more than to be kept waiting – particularly if it is due to someone's inefficiency. The Ox can be a hard taskmaster!

Once settled in a job or house the Ox will quite happily remain there for many years. He does not like change and he is also not particularly keen on travel. He does, however, enjoy gardening and other outdoor pursuits and he will often spend much of his spare time out of doors. The Ox is usually an excellent gardener and whenever possible he will always make sure he has a large area of ground to maintain. He usually prefers to live in the country than the town.

Due to his dedicated and dependable nature, the Ox will usually do well in his chosen career, providing he is given enough freedom to act on his own initiative. He invariably does well in politics, agriculture and in careers which need specialized training. The Ox is also very gifted in the arts and many Oxen have enjoyed considerable success as musicians or composers.

The Ox is not as outgoing as some and it often takes him a long time to establish friendships and feel relaxed in another person's company. His courtships are likely to be long, but once he is settled he will remain devoted and loyal to his partner. The Ox is particularly well-suited to those born under the signs of the Rat, Rabbit, Snake and Rooster. He can also establish a good relationship with the Monkey, Dog, Pig and another Ox, but he will find that he has little in common with the whimsical and sensitive Goat. He will also find it difficult to get on with the Horse, Dragon and Tiger – the Ox prefers a quiet and peaceful existence and those born under these three signs tend to be a little too lively and impulsive for his liking.

The female Ox has a kind and caring nature, and her home and family are very much her pride and joy. She always tries to do her best for her partner and can be a most conscientious and loving parent. She is an excellent organizer and also a very determined person who will often succeed in getting what she wants in life. She usually has a deep interest in the arts and is often a talented artist or musician.

The Ox is a very down-to-earth character. He is sincere, loyal and unpretentious. He can, however, be rather reserved and to some he may appear distant and aloof. He has a quiet nature, but underneath he is very strong-willed and ambitious. He has the courage of his convictions and is often prepared to stand up for what he believes is right, regardless of the consequences. He inspires confidence and trust and throughout his life he will rarely be short of people who are ready to support him or who admire his strong and resolute manner.

THE FIVE DIFFERENT TYPES OF OX

In addition to the 12 signs of the Chinese zodiac, there are five elements and these have a strengthening or moderating influence on the sign. The effects of the five elements on the Ox are described below, together with the years in which the elements were exercising their influence. Therefore all Oxen born in 1901 and 1961 are Metal Oxen, those born in 1913 and 1973 are Water Oxen, and so on.

Metal Ox: 1901, 1961
This Ox is confident and very strong-willed. He can be blunt and forthright in his views and is not afraid of speaking his mind. He sets about his objectives with a dogged determination, but he can become so wrapped up in his various activities that he can be oblivious to the thoughts and feelings of those around him, and this can sometimes be to his detriment. He is honest and dependable and will never promise more than he can deliver. He has a good appreciation of the arts and usually has a small circle of very good and loyal friends.

Water Ox: 1913, 1973
This Ox has a sharp and penetrating mind. He is a good organizer and sets about his work in a methodical manner. He is not as narrow-minded as some of the other types of Oxen and is more willing to involve others in his plans and aspirations. He usually has very high moral standards and is often attracted to careers in public service. He is a good

judge of character and has such a friendly and persuasive manner that he usually experiences little difficulty in securing his objectives. He is popular and has an excellent way with children.

Wood Ox: 1925, 1985

The Wood Ox conducts himself with an air of dignity and authority and will often take a leading role in any enterprise in which he gets involved. He is very self-confident and is direct in his dealings with others. He does, however, have a quick temper and has no hesitation in speaking his mind. He has tremendous drive and willpower and has an extremely good memory. The Wood Ox is particularly loyal and devoted to the members of his family and has a most caring nature.

Fire Ox: 1937, 1997

The Fire Ox has a powerful and assertive personality and is a hard and conscientious worker. He holds strong views and has very little patience when things do not go his own way. He can also get carried away in the excitement of the moment and does not always take into account the views of those around him. He nevertheless has many leadership qualities and will often reach positions of power, eminence and wealth. He usually has a small group of loyal and close friends and is very devoted to his family.

Earth Ox: 1949

This Ox sets about everything he does in a sensible and level-headed manner. He is ambitious, but he is also realistic in his aims and is often prepared to work long hours in order to secure his objectives. He is shrewd in financial and business matters and is a very good judge of character. He has a quiet nature and is greatly admired for his sincerity and integrity. He is also very loyal to his family and friends and his views and opinions are often sought by others.

PROSPECTS FOR THE OX IN 1997

The Chinese New Year starts on 7 February 1997. Until then, the old year, the Year of the Rat, is still making its presence felt.

The Year of the Rat (19 February 1996 to 6 February 1997) will have been an active year for the Ox – sometimes a little too active for his liking! However, it will have been a constructive year and in what remains of it the Ox can accomplish much.

Although the Ox may not always relish change, over the Rat year he will have been given several opportunities to improve upon his position and many Oxen will have taken on additional responsibilities or been successful in obtaining a new and more interesting type of work. For those Oxen who are seeking work or are dissatisfied with what they do, there will still be chances for them to pursue, even in the last few weeks of the year. In many ways the Rat year is a year of positive change and the Ox would do well to take full advantage of the aspects that prevail. The Ox should also keep alert to all that is going on around him in December 1996 and January 1997, especially in work matters, as he could learn of something that could be to his advantage over the next year. He should also not to be too independent in his actions at this time; those around him do want him to make the most of his many abilities and it would be in his interests to be more forthcoming when discussing his ideas and plans.

In addition to the progress that the Ox can make in his work, both his domestic and social life will bring him much satisfaction. His social life in particular will be busier in the closing stages of the year than it has been for a long time. The aspects are also excellent for romance and for those Oxen who are unattached and seeking new friends there will be some splendid opportunities for meeting others. A friendship started in the Rat year could well flourish in the next Chinese year.

Generally, the Rat year favours the Ox and while not all its events will have been entirely of his choosing, he will still have much to show for his efforts. However, the year will have been a demanding one for him and it would certainly be in his interests to give himself the opportunity to relax and unwind over the Christmas and New Year holidays. Suitably rested, he can then look forward to the favourable trends that prevail in his own year.

The Year of the Ox starts on 7 February and will be a most satisfactory year for the Ox. He will find it easier to plan his activities and be able to set about things in his own way rather than having to adapt to ever-changing circumstances. This will be a smoother and in some ways less active year for him and this is something he will much appreciate.

For those Oxen who have recently changed their work or been given more responsibilities, the Ox year will be a year in which they can consolidate their position and set about their new duties in earnest. The Ox, by being his usual thorough self, will find his work and accomplishments will be truly valued by his colleagues. Many Oxen will also find that they will be given greater freedom to pursue their plans and ideas and again this will be something they will appreciate.

Those Oxen seeking work or wanting to expand on their experience should not only remain alert for openings to pursue, particularly in the months of February to April, but also see whether they are eligible for any training courses. If so, they should actively follow these up; anything that the Ox can do to widen his experience will be very much to his advantage, not only for this year but also for the next few years as well.

Those Oxen involved in education are also likely to make good progress and while there will be times when they feel under considerable pressure, their hard work and diligence will be reflected in their results and the progress they make. Also, if these Oxen have not thought about which line of work they would like to enter, this would be a good year to do so and perhaps select some subjects in which to specialize. As far as academic matters and plans for the future are concerned, 1997 could prove a highly significant year. These Oxen will also obtain much assistance and encouragement by talking to those suitably qualified to advise.

The Ox will also enjoy a noticeable improvement in his financial situation this year. Generally he is careful in money matters, but if he does intend to make a sizeable purchase or investment over the year, it would be in his interests to check the small print first and be aware of any obligations he might be placed under. While financial matters are generally well aspected, a niggling matter involving his financial dealings could occur and without care this could take some time to resolve.

Travel will also figure prominently in 1997 and the Ox will enjoy any holidays and short breaks he takes. Even those Oxen who are not keen travellers should make sure that they do get away at least once over the year. All Oxen will benefit from a change of scene and many will find the destination they have chosen both interesting and enjoyable. Also, if the Ox has been longing to visit a certain place for some time or intending to visit friends or relations living some distance away, this would be an excellent year to do so.

However, while work, finance and travel are well aspected, undoubtedly the most auspicious area concerns the Ox's personal life. For the single and unattached Ox, this is a year for meeting others, for romance and marriage. It is also a splendid year for family matters and many Oxen will see an addition to their family or, for the older Oxen, be involved in a family celebration, possibly the marriage of a close relation or the birth of a grandchild. There will be some very good reasons for the Ox to feel justifiably proud over the year and personal and family matters will bring him much happiness. His family and those around him will also be most supportive and

although the Ox does have a tendency to keep his thoughts
to himself, it would be very much in his interests to be
more prepared to discuss his thoughts and ideas with those
close to him.

On a social level too, there will be much for the Ox to
enjoy. Many Oxen will attend pleasurable social occasions
over the year, particularly in the early summer months.
These will give the Ox many opportunities to add to his
circle of friends and acquaintances. Someone he meets in
the spring months could prove most helpful to him as the
year develops.

Generally, 1997 will be a productive year for the Ox but
even in the best years problems do still arise. In 1997 these
are most likely to concern bureaucratic matters and the
Ox does need to pay close attention to any important
forms and correspondence he receives, particularly when
concerned with matters of finance. The other possible
problem area could stem from a relatively trivial incident.
The Ox is one who has very set views and if he should
have a difference of opinion with someone he should, as
far as possible, aim to resolve the matter as quickly and
amicably as he can, even if it is just a case of 'agreeing to
disagree'. To let any disagreement continue and possibly
escalate could mar what will be a positive year for him as
well as distract him from more worthwhile activities. If the
Ox heeds this advice then this can be a most successful
year for him. It is, after all, his own year and one he will,
in time, come to look back on with pride and a genuine
sense of achievement.

As far as the different types of Ox are concerned, 1997 will be a positive year for the *Metal Ox*. He is blessed with a determined and thorough nature and often has very set objectives. In 1997 he will go a long way towards achieving – and even attain – some of these objectives. This is a most constructive year for him and by continuing to set about his activities in a purposeful way he can accomplish much. In his work he will make great strides. His ideas and plans will find favour with others and many Metal Oxen will find their endeavours rewarded with greater responsibilities, promotion or the opportunity to move to a different and better position. The first few months of the Ox year will be particularly important for career matters and at this time all Metal Oxen should remain alert for ways in which they can improve their present position. Also, should the Metal Ox find himself in a dilemma over what action or decision to take, particularly involving career matters, he should think the matter over carefully rather than taking hurried action. Time is on his side and he will be generally pleased with how the decisions he eventually does take work out for him. The Metal Ox will fare well in financial matters and, while usually conservative in his spending, he will spend much on his home in 1997. Many Metal Oxen will have extensive redecoration or improvements carried out and while this may result in more disruption than originally anticipated, the Metal Ox will be well pleased with the finished result. His domestic life will also give him much contentment and he will play a valuable and supportive role in the activities of those around him. Generally, family and personal activities will go well, although there is one word of warning. In 1997 the Metal

Ox should guard against being too demanding of others. Although he may have set views, he must accept that not all may share them and a too inflexible an attitude could lead to disagreements and take the edge off what will generally be a good domestic year. Also, as this will be a busy year for the Metal Ox, he should make sure that he sets a regular time aside for recreational pursuits and gives himself the chance to regularly relax and unwind. If not he could become tired, possibly irritable and not make as much of himself or the year as he could. If he keeps this in mind this can, however, be a positive and fulfilling year for him.

The *Water Ox* will enjoy 1997 and, provided he sets about his activities in his usual methodical way, will make good progress in almost all that he does. In his work he will consolidate any recent gains he has made and will do much to impress and gain the respect of others. Many Water Oxen will be able to advance their position over the year or transfer to new responsibilities which will allow them to usefully widen their experience. Although the Water Ox often has clear ideas about what he wishes to attain, he should show a certain flexibility with his plans. To remain intransigent or unduly stubborn over a career matter could deny him a valuable learning opportunity. In addition, the Water Ox will also get much benefit from any training courses that he is able to go on and, for those Water Oxen seeking work, it would be to their advantage to add to their skills over the year, even if it means learning something by themselves! By being adaptable and positive the Water Ox can make good gains over the year as well as prepare himself for the further advances he will make both in this and later years. The Water Ox will also fare well in financial matters and many will enjoy a noticeable improvement in their financial situation. However, if the Water Ox becomes involved in a major expense over the year, he should make sure that he makes allowances for this in his budget and, if need be, modifies some of his regular outgoings. He should also be wary of any speculative ventures that he hears about; all is not as straightforward as it might appear! The Water Ox's personal life will, however, be both happy and memorable. Many Water Oxen will have good reason for a personal celebration over the year and some will see an addition to their family. Admittedly there may be times in the Water Ox's domestic life when he will despair of all he has to do, but despite the pressures, these will still be enjoyable and fulfilling times for him. He can also look forward to a pleasurable social life and, for the unattached Water Ox, the prospects for making new friends, for romance and marriage are excellent. The spring and autumn months in particular will be an active and enjoyable time for him.

This will be a busy but positive year for the *Wood Ox*. For some time he may have considered moving or having some work carried out on his accommodation and this would be a good year to proceed with his plans. Those Water Oxen who move will feel particularly content with their new accommodation and will enjoy discovering the amenities in the area they move to as well as having the opportunity to establish a new social life. Admittedly the moving process will cause a period of disruption, but the Wood Ox will feel the effort worthwhile. Alternatively, many Wood Oxen will have some alterations carried out on their accommodation and again, despite a short period of upheaval, they will be pleased with the finished result. The Wood Ox will also take much delight in carrying out some practical projects over the year and, for DIY enthusiasts, this will prove a satisfying year. However, in his undertakings, the Wood Ox should not take risks with his physical well-being. He should seek help if he has to move heavy or cumbersome items and should follow safety instructions when engaged in hazardous tasks. Much of the activity that does occur over the year will take place in the first six months, with the second half being the more settled and enjoyable time. However, even though some of the year will be busy, the Wood Ox should make sure he does not neglect his own interests; he will find his hobbies a good source of relaxation for him as well as providing him with many hours of pleasure. He will also enjoy any breaks and holidays he is able to take and all Wood Oxen should try to ensure that they go away at least once over the year. Those Wood Oxen involved in education will make pleasing progress and, while some of what they are given to do will prove daunting and challenging, what they learn over the year will serve them well in the future. They could also find a new subject they take up of particular interest, so much so that it could prove relevant to the vocation they select in later life. Throughout the year the Wood Ox's family and friends will be most supportive and if he feels in need of any advice or additional help he should not hesitate to ask. His social life too will be most pleasurable and if at any time he feels lonely and in need of company it would be very much in his interests to go out more and perhaps join a club or local society. He will be glad he has made the effort, particularly as the aspects are so favourable for social matters. Generally, this will be a constructive year for the Wood Ox and while he may find some months disruptive and tiring, he will have good reason to be pleased with his achievements.

This is a year that holds considerable potential for the *Fire Ox*. However, to maximize the favourable trends that exist, he needs to sort out his priorities for the year and give himself some objectives to aim for. These can include household projects, his work, hobbies or, indeed, moving, but by deciding what he wants and working purposefully towards that aim the Fire Ox can achieve much. Without any such plan, however, he could let some excellent opportunities slip by or pass from activity to activity without achieving as much as he otherwise could. Overall, 1997 can be a most constructive year, but it does call on the Fire Ox to give of his best and use his time wisely. Those Fire Oxen in work will have a particularly significant year. Some will take on more responsibilities while others will retire; either way the Fire Ox will be satisfied with how events go for him and he will also find his past efforts will be recognized and rewarded. Financially, too, the Fire Ox will fare well and end the year in a much improved position. However, while the Fire Ox is usually cautious in financial matters, he must exercise care if he intends to enter into any sizeable transaction or investment over the year. He should make sure he is conversant with any obligations he might be placed under and, if he has any doubts, should seek further advice. Financial matters will go well, but the Fire Ox must avoid taking risks or becoming complacent in money matters. Domestically, this will be a settled and content year and the Fire Ox can look forward to having some pleasing times with his family. In particular he would do well to encourage joint projects around the home as these will give all concerned much satisfaction. The Fire Ox should also aim to go out more over the year; he could find joining a local society or organization especially pleasurable as well as providing him with an additional interest. This particularly applies to those Fire Oxen who may have been feeling lonely or had some recent adversity to cope with. The Fire Ox will also benefit from any breaks and holidays that he is able to take over the year; generally, travel is favourably aspected. Overall, this will be a satisfying year for the Fire Ox, but to benefit from the positive trends that exist he does need to give some thought to what he actually wants to accomplish over the year. By using his time wisely, this can be both a fulfilling and enjoyable year for him.

This will be a satisfying year for the *Earth Ox*. He will be able to make steady progress in most of his activities as well as have some enjoyable times with his family and friends. In his work he will continue to impress and will be given the opportunity to move to more interesting and rewarding duties. Similarly, many Earth Oxen who are seeking work or wanting to expand on their experience will be successful in obtaining another, more challenging position. When the Earth Ox has set his mind on attaining something he works until he has achieved what he wants and this will be the pattern over the year. He will find bold, positive and determined action will bring results – and this year they will be the results he wants! Those around him will be supportive and encouraging and he should experience little opposition to his plans or ideas. However, while he knows in his own mind what he wants to achieve, he should still listen closely to any advice he is given, particularly from those who speak with experience. There will be much wisdom in what he is told. Financial matters will go well for the Earth Ox and early in the year he could be successful in buying some items for his home at some most favourable prices. It would certainly be in his interests to keep alert for bargains at sale times. Travel is also well aspected and the Earth Ox should take advantage of any opportunity he gets to visit places or areas that he has wanted to visit for some time. Domestically and socially, the year will bring him much pleasure; however, he should try to avoid becoming so preoccupied with his own concerns that he does not pay as much attention to what is going on around him as he should. If he is not careful, tensions could so easily arise and spoil what will otherwise be a successful year for him. The Earth Ox should also make sure that he sets a regular time aside for his own interests and recreational pursuits. Even though he may feel there are more pressing things he should do, his hobbies do provide him with an important source of relaxation and give him a break from his everyday concerns. If the Earth Ox bears these points in mind, this will be both a successful and pleasant year for him.

FAMOUS OXEN

Martin Amis, Hans Christian Andersen, Johann Sebastian Bach, Warren Beatty, Menachem Begin, Tony Benn, Jon

Bon Jovi, Napoleon Bonaparte, Jim Bowen, Rory Bremner, Jeff Bridges, Benjamin Britten, Frank Bruno, Richard Burton, Barbara Bush, Johnny Carson, Barbara Cartland, Judith Chalmers, Charlie Chaplin, Warren Christopher, George Cole, Natalie Cole, Peter Cook, Bill Cosby, Tom Courtenay, Tony Curtis, Sammy Davis Jr, Jacques Delors, Donald Dewar, Walt Disney, Patrick Duffy, Harry Enfield, Jane Fonda, Michael Foot, Gerald Ford, Edward Fox, Michael J. Fox, Peter Gabriel, Richard Gere, Ryan Giggs, Whoopi Goldberg, William Hague, George Frederick Handel, Robert Hardy, King Harold V of Norway, Nigel Havers, Mariel Hemingway, Adolf Hitler, Dustin Hoffman, Anthony Hopkins, Saddam Hussein, Billy Joel, Don Johnson, Jack Jones, King Juan Carlos of Spain, Penny Junor, B. B. King, Mark Knopfler, Burt Lancaster, k. d. Lang, Jessica Lange, Angela Lansbury, Jack Lemmon, Nicholas Lyndhurst, Kate Moss, Alison Moyet, Eddie Murphy, Jawaharlal Nehru, Paul Newman, Jack Nicholson, Leslie Nielsen, Billy Ocean, Oscar Peterson, Colin Powell, Robert Redford, Jamie Redknapp, Peter Paul Rubens, Willie Rushton, Meg Ryan, Arthur Scargill, Monica Seles, Peter Sellers, Jean Sibelius, Jimmy Somerville, Sissy Spacek, Bruce Springsteen, Rod Steiger, Meryl Streep, Elaine Stritch, Chris Sutton, Loretta Swit, Lady Thatcher, Mel Torme, Scott F. Turow, Twiggy, Mary Tyler Moore, Dick Van Dyke, the Princess of Wales, Zoë Wanamaker, Tom Watson, the Duke of Wellington, Alan Whicker, Barbara Windsor, Ernie Wise, W. B. Yeats.

8 FEBRUARY 1902 ∿ 28 JANUARY 1903		*Water Tiger*
26 JANUARY 1914 ∿ 13 FEBRUARY 1915		*Wood Tiger*
13 FEBRUARY 1926 ∿ 1 FEBRUARY 1927		*Fire Tiger*
31 JANUARY 1938 ∿ 18 FEBRUARY 1939		*Earth Tiger*
17 FEBRUARY 1950 ∿ 5 FEBRUARY 1951		*Metal Tiger*
5 FEBRUARY 1962 ∿ 24 JANUARY 1963		*Water Tiger*
23 JANUARY 1974 ∿ 10 FEBRUARY 1975		*Wood Tiger*
9 FEBRUARY 1986 ∿ 28 JANUARY 1987		*Fire Tiger*

THE
TIGER

THE PERSONALITY OF THE TIGER

Most roads lead men homewards,
My road leads me forth.

– *John Masefield: a Tiger*

The Tiger is born under the sign of courage. He is a charismatic figure and usually holds very firm views and beliefs. He is strong-willed and determined, and sets about most of the things he does with a tremendous energy and enthusiasm. He is very alert and quick-witted and his mind is forever active. He is a highly original thinker and is nearly always brimming with new ideas or full of enthusiasm for some new project or scheme.

The Tiger adores challenges and loves to get involved in anything which he thinks has an exciting future or which catches his imagination. He is prepared to take risks and does not like to be bound either by convention or the dictates of others. The Tiger likes to be free to act as he chooses and at least once during his life he will throw caution to the wind and go off and do the things he wants to do.

The Tiger does, however, have a somewhat restless nature. Even though he is often prepared to throw himself wholeheartedly into a project, his initial enthusiasm can soon wane if he sees something more appealing. He can also be rather impulsive and there will be occasions in his life when he acts in a manner which he later regrets. If the Tiger were to think things out or to persevere in his various activities, he would almost certainly enjoy a greater degree of success.

Fortunately, the Tiger is lucky in most of his enterprises, but should things not work out as he had hoped, he is liable to suffer from severe bouts of depression and it will often take him a long time to recover. His life often consists of a series of ups and downs.

The Tiger is, however, very adaptable. He has an adventurous spirit and rarely stays in the same place for long. In the early stages of his life he is likely to try his hand at several different jobs and he will also change his residence fairly frequently.

The Tiger is very honest and open in his dealings with others. He hates any sort of hypocrisy or falsehood. He is also well known for being blunt and forthright and has no hesitation in speaking his mind. He can also be most rebellious at times, particularly against any form of petty authority, and while this can lead the Tiger into conflict with others, he is never one to shrink from an argument or avoid standing up for what he believes is right.

The Tiger is a natural leader and can invariably rise to the top of his chosen profession. He does not, however, care for anything too bureaucratic or detailed and he also does not like to obey orders. He can be stubborn and obstinate, and throughout his life he likes to retain a certain amount of independence in his actions and be responsible to no one but himself. He likes to consider that all his achievements are due to his own efforts and unless he cannot avoid it, he will rarely ask for support from others.

Ironically, despite his self-confidence and leadership qualities, the Tiger can be indecisive and will often delay making a major decision until the very last moment. He can also be sensitive to criticism.

Although the Tiger is capable of earning large sums of money, he is rather a spendthrift and does not always put his money to its best use. He can also be most generous and will often shower lavish gifts on friends and relations.

The Tiger cares very much for his reputation and the image that he tries to project. He carries himself with an air of dignity and authority and enjoys being the centre of attention. He is very adept at attracting publicity, both for himself and for the causes he supports.

The Tiger often marries young and he will find himself best suited to those born under the signs of the Pig, Dog, Horse and Goat. He can also get on well with the Rat, Rabbit and Rooster, but will find the Ox and Snake a bit too quiet and too serious for his liking, and he will also be highly irritated by the Monkey's rather mischievous and inquisitive ways. The Tiger will also find it difficult to get on with another Tiger or a Dragon – both partners will want to dominate the relationship and could find it difficult to compromise on even the smallest of matters.

The Tigress is lively, witty and a marvellous hostess at parties. She is usually most attractive and takes great care over her appearance. She can also be a very doting mother and while she believes in letting her children have their freedom, she makes an excellent teacher and will ensure that her children are brought up well and want for nothing. Like her male counterpart, she has numerous interests and likes to have sufficient independence and freedom to go off and do the things that she wants to do. She also has a most caring and generous nature.

The Tiger has many commendable qualities. He is honest, courageous and often a source of inspiration for others. Providing he can curb the wilder excesses of his restless nature, he is almost certain to lead a most fulfilling and satisfying life.

THE FIVE DIFFERENT TYPES OF TIGER

In addition to the 12 signs of the Chinese zodiac, there are five elements and these have a strengthening or moderating influence on the sign. The effects of the five elements on the Tiger are described below, together with the years in which the elements were exercising their influence. Therefore all Tigers born in 1950 are Metal Tigers, those born in 1902 and 1962 are Water Tigers, and so on.

Metal Tiger: 1950
The Metal Tiger has an assertive and outgoing personality. He is very ambitious and, while his aims may change from time to time, he will work relentlessly until he has obtained what he wants. He can, however, be impatient for results and also get highly strung if things do not work out as he would like. He is distinctive in his appearance and is admired and respected by many.

Water Tiger: 1902, 1962

This Tiger has a wide variety of interests and is always eager to experiment with new ideas or go off and explore distant lands. He is versatile, shrewd and has a kindly nature. The Water Tiger tends to remain calm in a crisis, although he can be annoyingly indecisive at times. He communicates well with others and through his many capabilities and persuasive nature he usually achieves what he wants in life. He is also highly imaginative and is often a gifted orator or writer.

Wood Tiger: 1914, 1974

The Wood Tiger has a very friendly and pleasant personality. He is less independent than some of the other types of Tiger and is more prepared to work with others to secure a desired objective. However, he does have a tendency to jump from one thing to another and can get easily distracted. He is usually very popular, has a large circle of friends and invariably leads a busy and enjoyable social life. He also has a good sense of humour.

Fire Tiger: 1926, 1986

The Fire Tiger sets about everything he does with great verve and enthusiasm. He loves action and is always ready to throw himself wholeheartedly into anything which catches his imagination. He has many leadership qualities and is capable of communicating his ideas and enthusiasm to others. He is very much an optimist and can be most generous. He has a likeable nature and can be a witty and persuasive speaker.

Earth Tiger: 1938

This Tiger is responsible and level-headed. He studies everything objectively and tries to be scrupulously fair in all his dealings. Unlike other Tigers, he is prepared to specialize in certain areas rather than get distracted by other matters, but he can become so involved with what he is doing that he does not always take into account the views and opinions of those around him. He has good business sense and is usually very successful in later life. He has a large circle of friends and pays great attention to both his appearance and his reputation.

PROSPECTS FOR THE TIGER IN 1997

The Chinese New Year starts on 7 February 1997. Until then, the old year, the Year of the Rat, is still making its presence felt.

The Year of the Rat (19 February 1996 to 6 February 1997) will have been a variable year for the Tiger and, while he will have made some progress, this will not have been without considerable effort on his part. For what remains of the Rat year the Tiger needs to proceed carefully and concentrate his efforts on specific matters rather than spread his energies too widely. He would also do well to act in conjunction with others rather than maintain too independent an attitude, as some Tigers can be apt to do. The Rat year is a year for restraint and modest rather than swift progress.

In financial matters, too, the Tiger will need to be prudent and as the Rat year ends he would do well to keep a watch over his general level of spending. To deplete his resources too far could result in him having to budget carefully in the first few months of next year.

More favourably aspected, though, is the Tiger's domestic and social life. In the last few months of the Rat year the Tiger can look forward to some enjoyable times with his family and friends as well as attending some memorable functions. December will be an especially favourable month and the Christmas and New Year holidays will not only be a generally pleasant time for the Tiger but will also give him a chance to unwind after the pressures of the year. He will also thoroughly enjoy any travelling that he undertakes at this time and, if he gets the opportunity to meet up with friends or relations he has not seen for some time, he should do so. Such a meeting will give all concerned much pleasure.

January 1997 will be a significant month for the Tiger and he would do well to keep alert to all that is going on around him and look out for new opportunities as well as deal promptly with any important correspondence he receives. Some of what happens in January 1997 could have far-reaching consequences.

The Year of the Ox starts on 7 February and is going to be an important but challenging year for the Tiger. In 1997 he can make headway in many of his activities but the year will not be without its difficulties. However, while there are negative aspects, there is much that the Tiger can do to overcome them and, if he proceeds with care, he can enjoy a reasonable year. Furthermore, what he does accomplish in the Ox year will help prepare him for the considerably better times that await him in 1998, his own year.

In 1997, however, the Tiger does need to keep a tight rein over his impulsive and somewhat restless nature. This is not a year for taking risks or for acting without the support of others. Indeed, to get the best from the year, no matter what area of his life it might concern, the Tiger needs to plan, sort out his priorities and then work purposefully towards his objectives. The progress he makes will come from careful planning and concentrated effort.

In his work the Tiger would do best to concentrate on areas in which he has most experience and can best use his skills. This is not a year for starting ambitious new projects or for taking undue risks. However, the Tiger's alert and diligent manner will impress others and this will hold him in good stead for the future. Similarly, any additional experience he can gain in the Ox year, either by enrolling on courses or by private study, will be in his interests. For many Tigers, what they learn and accomplish in 1997 will prepare the way for the considerably better times that lie in the near future.

Throughout the year the Tiger does, however, need to pay close attention to the views of his colleagues and should refrain from being too independent in his actions. Also, should he find himself in a fraught situation, he should think carefully before he speaks. If not, his remarks could become misconstrued and undermine some of the goodwill he has built up. This is a year for diplomacy and tact – something that not all Tigers find easy!

Any Tiger seeking work or wanting to change his present duties should remain alert for opportunities to pursue, especially in the early months of the year. While he may not always be successful in getting the sort of position he seeks, any position that he does obtain will usefully broaden his experience and open up opportunities that might not have been available before.

Another area in which the Tiger needs to exercise care is when dealing with finance. Over the year he should be wary about spending large amounts of money on the spur of the moment and he would also do well to keep his some-times overly generous nature in check. This is not a year in which he can afford to be either too extravagant or indul-gent – if he is, he could find any savings he has had to dip into will be hard to replenish. Also, without a certain restraint, he could find himself having to cut down on his spending later in the year and having to deny himself items he would like. As with most areas in 1997, in finance, the Tiger can negate the more adverse aspects that prevail by being careful and cautious.

More positively, however, the Tiger can look forward to some pleasing times with his family and friends. His domestic life will give him much satisfaction and he will delight in the progress and achievements made by those dear to him. Any further encouragement and support he feels able to give will be much appreciated; probably more so than he may realize at the time. However, in his domestic life the Tiger does need to remain mindful of the feelings of those around him and if some of his plans and ideas do not quite meet with their approval he should accept this rather than proceed regardless. In 1997 he will get much useful and pertinent advice from his loved ones and should pay close attention to their views and the advice they give him. They do have his best interests at heart.

Socially, too, the year will contain some pleasurable times

and the Tiger can look forward to attending several memorable events as the year progresses. At one, in the summer, he could easily find himself the centre of attention!

There will be several romantic opportunities for the unattached Tiger, although it would be in his interests to let any new friendship develop gradually rather than rush into a major commitment. This way the friendship will be based upon a more secure and stable foundation. The months from April to June could be particularly meaningful for the unattached Tiger.

The Tiger should also make sure that he sets a regular time aside for his own interests over the year and he could find out-of-door activities especially enjoyable. His travels in 1997 will also go well and one journey, arranged at short notice and to a rather unusual destination, could prove particularly memorable. All Tigers should try to go away at least once over the year – the holidays and breaks that they take will prove most beneficial and travel is certainly one of the areas which is more favourably aspected.

Another area which will give the Tiger much satisfaction involves improvements and alterations that he carries out on his home and garden. The Tiger will find practical projects will go well and both he and those around him will be well pleased with household and garden projects undertaken over the year.

The Tiger is blessed with many fine abilities and is highly regarded by those around him. With his personable nature and inventive mind he has much in his favour. But in 1997 some of his qualities will be tested and not all the activities that he engages in will proceed as smoothly or as quickly as he would like. For the Tiger, so keen to give of his best, some of the year could prove frustrating. However, providing he remains careful in his undertakings, he will be preparing the way for the considerably better times that lie ahead. From October onwards the Tiger will notice a gradual improvement in his fortunes and this will gather pace as the Ox year draws to a close. Also, his accomplishments over the year and the experience he gains will certainly benefit him in the more favourable times that will soon come his way.

As far as the different types of Tiger are concerned, 1997 will be an important year for the *Metal Tiger*. Although the year will not be without its difficulties, he will still be able to accomplish much. The Metal Tiger is blessed with a determined and ambitious nature and this will help him considerably over the year. While lesser signs may give up when faced with problems and delays, the Metal Tiger keeps going, and it is his perseverance and strong will that will enable him to make progress during the year. Early in 1997 he should decide upon his priorities and then work purposefully towards attaining them. He should, however, be realistic in his aims and avoid the temptation of taking on too many commitments at any one time. This is a year when concentrated effort on particular goals will bring results. Many Metal Tigers will find that what they do achieve over the year will lead to their being given greater responsibilities later in the year or will place them in an excellent position to make further advancement next year. Any Metal Tigers seeking work or wanting a change in their duties could be successful in gaining a position completely different from anything they have done before.

Although this might prove daunting at first, the enterprising Metal Tiger will rise to the challenge it gives him and discover talents and strengths he never realized he possessed! The Metal Tiger's domestic life will be busy and while those around him will place many demands on him, he will obtain much satisfaction and pleasure from his home life. He should, however, make every effort to share his ideas and views with those around him as well as discuss any concerns he might have. Throughout the year he will be grateful for the encouragement and advice he is given. The Metal Tiger may not always have as much time for his social life or his interests as he would like, but it is important he does not neglect these; they do provide a valuable source of relaxation and enjoyment for him as well as give him a rest from everyday duties. The Metal Tiger should also make sure he has a proper break or holiday over the year; a change of scene will prove most beneficial for him and the travel that he does undertake will go well. Generally, if the Metal Tiger decides upon his priorities for the year and is not overly ambitious in what he attempts, he can make pleasing progress. What he achieves over the year will help prepare him for the excellent advances he will make in 1998.

Although the Ox year may not be the easiest of years for the Tiger, it is still one which holds much potential for the *Water Tiger*. He is both shrewd and perceptive and has a skilful knack of choosing the right moment to advance his ideas or proceed with his plans. He also has a most persuasive manner and this will serve him well. Although much of the year will be quiet and will allow the Water Tiger to consolidate any gains he has made in recent years, when he does spot an opening to pursue – especially in his work – he should be quick to act and stands a favourable chance of success. Admittedly the opportunities may not be plentiful, but when they do occur the Water Tiger will certainly make the most of them. June in particular could be a most active month. Throughout the year, however, the Water Tiger should continue to set about his activities in his usual diligent way but at the same time be prepared to work in close co-operation with others rather than adopt too independent an attitude. Neither should he take unnecessary risks nor proceed with any new undertaking without making sure he has the support of others. While the Water Tiger will make progress over the year, this is not a time when he can act single-handed. He would also do well to go on any courses which he might be eligible for and, if there is a qualification he considers might be useful, he would do well to investigate further. Anything positive he can do to add to his skills will do much to enhance his prospects both for later in the year and for 1998. The Water Tiger does, however, need to exercise caution in financial matters and if he gets involved in any large expenses he should make sure he makes allowances for these in his budget. Generally, this is not a year when he should stretch his resources too far. His domestic life will be busy over the year but those around him will be a source of considerable pride to him. He will also be encouraged by the support he is given and would do well to heed any advice he receives, particularly from a more senior relation. The Water Tiger will also delight in some home improvements that he carries out, although he could find these will take him more time and be more involved than he initially anticipated. He will also obtain much benefit from any holidays that he takes and, with the various demands that he will be under during 1997, it is important that he sets a regular time aside for his hobbies and interests. Out-of-door activities in particular will do him much good. Generally the Water Tiger will fare reasonably well in the Ox year and what he accomplishes will do much to lay the foundation for the significant progress he will make over the next year.

This will be an interesting year for the *Wood Tiger* and while there will be parts of the year he will greatly enjoy, there will be other parts which will prove challenging. Generally, however, he will get greatest pleasure from his personal and domestic life. Those close to him will be loving and supportive and he can look forward to some personally happy and memorable times. He will also delight in some joint projects that he undertakes, especially if he has recently moved or is in the process of setting up a home. Domestically, the year will be active but fulfilling. His social life too will be generally pleasurable and for the unattached Wood Tiger there will be several excellent opportunities to establish new friendships, particularly in the first few months of the Ox year. However, while this area of his life will go well for him, there are other areas that could prove troublesome. In 1997 the Wood Tiger needs to exercise great care when dealing with financial matters and if he enters into any large transaction he should make sure he is aware of any obligations he is being placed under. If he has doubts over any financial matter he would do well to check rather than take risks. It would also be in his interests to watch his level of spending. This is not a year in which he can afford to be too extravagant or complacent in financial matters. Also, in his work, events may not always go smoothly. Over the year he could find it difficult to make as much progress as he would like or that his plans do not quite work out in the manner he had hoped. For one so capable and ambitious, the Ox year could prove a little frustrating. However, the Wood Tiger can take heart. By continuing to set about his duties in his conscientious manner he will be adding to his experience as well as impressing those more senior to himself; all this will help the Wood Tiger later in the year and throughout 1998, when he will start to make the career advances he has been aiming for. In many respects, 1997 is a year in which the Wood Tiger will be learning and preparing the way for the better times that lie ahead. Similarly, Wood Tigers seeking work or wanting to change their duties should actively follow up any openings they see. Although their efforts may not always meet with success, their perseverance will eventually pay off and usually at a time when they least expect it. Generally the Wood Tiger will notice a substantial upturn in his fortunes from October onwards and this will gather pace as the Tiger year approaches. The Ox year may not be the easiest for the Wood Tiger, but certainly, from a personal point of view, it will hold much happiness for him.

This will be a demanding year for the *Fire Tiger* and if he is to avoid problems and delays he will need to proceed carefully with most of his activities. For one so keen and ambitious, a cautious approach is not one that comes easily. However, if the Fire Tiger plans his activities well, concentrates on specific tasks and avoids being too hasty in his actions, then he will do much to negate the more awkward aspects that prevail. Fire Tigers involved in education, however, will cover some important work during the year and many will start a new subject which will prove significant to them in future years, possibly even becoming the basis of their vocation. There may be times when these Fire Tigers will feel daunted by what is being asked of them but, by working to the best of their abilities, they will acquit themselves well and will have every reason to be pleased with their progress. All Fire Tigers do, however, need to exercise caution in financial matters and particularly watch their level of spending. They should also be wary about impulse buying – to buy an expensive item on the spur of the moment could leave them later regretting their purchase or finding they could have done better elsewhere. Wherever possible the Fire Tiger needs to plan his major purchases carefully and makes sure he makes allowances for these in his budget. More positively, however, the Fire Tiger's personal life will give him much satisfaction. He can look forward to having some pleasurable times with his family and friends as well as attending some memorable and often unexpected social functions. He would do well, however, to remain mindful of the views and opinions of those around him and while there may be some matters on which he may disagree, he should not let these affect the normally excellent relations he has with others. In case of a difference of opinion, he should either seek a compromise or 'agree to disagree'. To remain intransigent or unduly stubborn could result in a needless souring of relations and this is something that he would do well to avoid. Those Fire Tigers who are seeking new friendships or who have had some problems to contend with in recent years should make every effort to go out more and possibly consider joining a local society. They will certainly be glad they made the effort and a new friendship they form could bring them considerable happiness. The Fire Tiger will also enjoy the travelling he undertakes over the year, especially in the early summer months. Generally, if he is realistic in his expectations and exercises care in his activities, this will prove a reasonable year for him and one which will contain some enjoyable times. But should he be tempted to take risks or over-commit himself, then problems might arise. This is a year when the Fire Tiger needs to be careful and on his guard.

This will be a variable year for the *Earth Tiger* and while it will hold some pleasant times for him, he could find it difficult to achieve as much as he would like. His plans could be subject to delay and alteration or he might feel that his efforts do not always bring him the results he desires. There will be times when the Earth Tiger will feel frustrated by his apparent lack of progress and this is not a year when he can expect rapid results or embark on ambitious new projects. However, if he concentrates his efforts on specific matters and acts in conjunction with others, then a certain amount of progress is possible. Throughout the year he should remain mindful of the views of those around him and show himself willing to adapt to new situations as they occur. To adopt too independent an attitude or be intransigent in the face of change could leave the Earth Tiger isolated as well as undermining his position. In 1997 he needs to proceed carefully and cautiously, particularly in work activities. Similarly, he should not take undue risks in financial matters and would do well to keep a close watch over his level of spending. Generally, his prospects will improve in the second half of the year and this is also the time when he should start to give some thought to his longer term future. In this he would do well to discuss his ideas with those around him and by the end of the year he will be well pleased with some of the decisions he has taken. Although 1997 may not be the easiest of years for him, some of the actions he takes will prove significant and will have a favourable bearing on the next few years. Domestically, the Earth Tiger can look forward to some enjoyable times with his family as well as take much delight in the progress of some younger members of his family. His social life, too, will be pleasant, particularly in the second half of the year. Travel is also favourably aspected and the Earth Tiger would do well to make sure he gets away at least once during the year. He will find any holidays he takes most beneficial for him and is likely to be well pleased with his choice of destination, particularly if it is somewhere he has never visited before. The Earth Tiger should also give serious thought to taking up a new hobby or interest over the year, possibly one that has intrigued him in the past but he has never had the time to follow up. He could find this will develop in a meaningful way over the next few years.

FAMOUS TIGERS

Sir David Attenborough, Queen Beatrix of the Netherlands, Ludwig van Beethoven, Tony Bennett, Tom Berenger, Chuck Berry, Richard Branson, Garth Brooks, Mel Brooks, Isambard Kingdom Brunel, Agatha Christie, David Coleman, Phil Collins, Jason Connery, Alan Coren, Gemma Craven, Tom Cruise, Paul Daniels, Emily Dickinson, David Dimbleby, Isadora Duncan, Dwight Eisenhower, Queen Elizabeth II, Enya, Roberta Flack, Frederick Forsyth, Jodie Foster, Connie Francis, Charles de Gaulle, Crystal Gayle, Susan George, Elliott Gould, Buddy Greco, Germaine Greer, Sir Alec Guinness, Naseem Hamed, Harriet Harman, Ed Harris, Thor Heyerdahl, Lord Howe, William Hurt, Derek Jacobi, Matthew Kelly, Sarah Kennedy, Dorothy Lamour, Stan Laurel, Ian McCaskill, Karl Marx, John Masefield, Marilyn Monroe, Demi Moore, Eric Morecambe, Lord Owen, Marco Polo, Jonathan Porritt, John Prescott, the Princess Royal, Oliver Reed, Diana Rigg, Lionel Ritchie, Kenny Rogers, Sir Jimmy Savile, Phillip Schofield, Dick Spring, Sir David Steel, Pamela Stephenson, Dame Joan Sutherland, Dylan Thomas, Terence Trent-D'Arby, Liv Ullman, Jon Voight, Julie Walters, Oscar Wilde, Tennessee Williams, Terry Wogan, Stevie Wonder, Natalie Wood.

29 JANUARY 1903 ～ 15 FEBRUARY 1904   *Water Rabbit*

14 FEBRUARY 1915 ～ 2 FEBRUARY 1916   *Wood Rabbit*

2 FEBRUARY 1927 ～ 22 JANUARY 1928   *Fire Rabbit*

19 FEBRUARY 1939 ～ 7 FEBRUARY 1940   *Earth Rabbit*

6 FEBRUARY 1951 ～ 26 JANUARY 1952   *Metal Rabbit*

25 JANUARY 1963 ～ 12 FEBRUARY 1964   *Water Rabbit*

11 FEBRUARY 1975 ～ 30 JANUARY 1976   *Wood Rabbit*

29 JANUARY 1987 ～ 16 FEBRUARY 1988   *Fire Rabbit*

THE
RABBIT

THE PERSONALITY OF THE RABBIT

There is no man, no woman, so small but that they
cannot make their life great by high endeavour.
                              – *Thomas Carlyle: a Rabbit*

The Rabbit is born under the signs of virtue and prudence.
He is intelligent, well-mannered and prefers a quiet and
peaceful existence. He dislikes any sort of unpleasantness
and will try to steer clear of arguments and disputes. He is
very much a pacifist and tends to have a calming influence
on those around him.

He has wide interests and usually has a good appreciation of the arts and the finer things in life. He also knows
how to enjoy himself and will often gravitate to the best
restaurants and night spots in town.

The Rabbit is a witty and intelligent speaker and loves
being involved in a good discussion. His views and advice
are often sought by others and he can be relied upon to be
discreet and diplomatic. He will rarely raise his voice in
anger and will even turn a blind eye to matters which
displease him just to preserve the peace. The Rabbit likes to
remain on good terms with everyone, but he can be rather
sensitive and takes any form of criticism very badly. He
will also be the first to get out of the way if he sees any
form of trouble brewing.

The Rabbit is a quiet and efficient worker and has an
extremely good memory. He is very astute in business and
financial matters, but his degree of success often depends
on the conditions that prevail. He hates being in a situation

which is fraught with tension or where he has to make quick and sudden decisions. Wherever possible he will plan his various activities with the utmost care and a good deal of caution. He does not like to take risks and does not take kindly to changes. Basically, he seeks a secure, calm and stable environment, and when conditions are right he is more than happy to leave things as they are.

The Rabbit is conscientious in most of the things he does and, because of his methodical and ever-watchful nature, can often do well in his chosen profession. He makes a good diplomat, lawyer, shopkeeper, administrator or priest and he excels in any job where he can use his superb skills as a communicator. He tends to be loyal to his employers and is respected for his integrity and honesty, but if he ever finds himself in a position of great power he can become rather intransigent and authoritarian.

The Rabbit attaches great importance to his home and will often spend much time and money to maintain and furnish it and to fit it with all the latest comforts – the Rabbit is very much a creature of comfort! He is also something of a collector and there are many Rabbits who derive much pleasure from collecting antiques, stamps, coins, *objets d'art* or anything else which catches their eye or particularly interests them.

The female Rabbit has a friendly, caring and considerate nature, and will do all in her power to give her home a happy and loving atmosphere. She is also very sociable and enjoys holding parties and entertaining. She has a great ability to make the maximum use of her time and, although she involves herself in numerous activities, she always manages to find time to sit back and enjoy a good read or a chat. She has a great sense of humour, is very artistic and is often a talented gardener.

The Rabbit takes considerable care over his appearance and is usually smart and very well turned out. He also attaches great importance to his relations with others and matters of the heart are particularly important to him. He will rarely be short of admirers and will often have several serious romances before he settles down. The Rabbit is not the most faithful of signs, but he will find that he is especially well-suited to those born under the signs of the Goat, Snake, Pig and Ox. Due to his sociable and easy-going manner he can also get on well with the Tiger, Dragon, Horse, Monkey, Dog and another Rabbit, but will feel ill at ease with the Rat and Rooster as both these signs tend to speak their mind and be critical in their comments, and the Rabbit just loathes any form of criticism or unpleasantness.

The Rabbit is usually lucky in life and often has the happy knack of being in the right place at the right time. He is talented and quick-witted, but he does sometimes put pleasure before work, and wherever possible will tend to opt for the easy life. He can at times be a little reserved and suspicious of the motives of others, but generally will lead a long and contented life and one which – as far as possible – will be free of strife and discord.

THE FIVE DIFFERENT TYPES
OF RABBIT

In addition to the 12 signs of the Chinese zodiac, there are five elements and these have a strengthening or moderating influence on the sign. The effects of the five elements on the Rabbit are described below, together with the years in which the elements were exercising their influence. Therefore all Rabbits born in 1951 are Metal Rabbits, those born in 1903 and 1963 are Water Rabbits, and so on.

Metal Rabbit: 1951
This Rabbit is capable, ambitious and has very definite views on what he wants to achieve in life. He can occasionally appear reserved and aloof, but this is mainly because he likes to keep his thoughts and ideas to himself. He has a very quick and alert mind and is particularly shrewd in business matters. He can also be very cunning in his actions. The Metal Rabbit has a good appreciation of the arts and likes to mix in the best circles. He usually has a small but very loyal group of friends.

Water Rabbit: 1903, 1963
The Water Rabbit is popular, intuitive and keenly aware of the feelings of those around him. He can, however, be rather sensitive and tends to take things too much to heart. He is very precise and thorough in everything he does and has an exceedingly good memory. He tends to be quiet and

at times rather withdrawn, but he expresses his ideas well and is highly regarded by his family, friends and colleagues.

Wood Rabbit: 1915, 1975

The Wood Rabbit is likeable, easy going and very adaptable. He prefers to work in groups rather than on his own and likes to have the support and encouragement of others. He can, however, be rather reticent in expressing his views and it would be in his own interests to become a little more open and forthright and let others know how he feels on certain matters. He usually has many friends and enjoys an active social life. He is noted for his generosity.

Fire Rabbit: 1927, 1987

The Fire Rabbit has a friendly, outgoing personality. He likes socializing and being on good terms with everyone. He is discreet and diplomatic and has a very good understanding of human nature. He is also strong-willed and provided he has the necessary backing and support he can go far in life. He does not, however, suffer adversity well and can become moody and depressed when things are not working out as he would like. The Fire Rabbit is very intuitive and there are some who are even noted for their psychic ability. The Fire Rabbit has a particularly good manner with children.

Earth Rabbit: 1939

The Earth Rabbit is a quiet individual, but he is nevertheless very shrewd and astute. He is realistic in his aims and
is prepared to work long and hard in order to achieve his
objectives. He has good business sense and is invariably
lucky in financial matters. He also has a most persuasive
manner and usually experiences little difficulty in getting
others to fall in with his plans. He is held in very high
esteem by his friends and colleagues and his views and
opinions are often sought and highly valued.

PROSPECTS FOR THE RABBIT IN 1997

The Chinese New Year starts on 7 February 1997. Until
then, the old year, the Year of the Rat, is still making its
presence felt.

The Year of the Rat (19 February 1996 to 6 February
1997) will have been a variable year for the Rabbit and, as
it draws to a close, he will still need to exercise care with
his undertakings.

In his work the Rabbit should be his usual vigilant self. He
should be wary of taking undue risks, of over-committing
himself or of placing too much credence on rumours or
gossip. Fortunately the Rabbit's perceptive nature will do
much to help, but he does need to be on his guard. Also, if
he feels under too much pressure, he should either seek
assistance or decide upon his priorities and concentrate on
these. With care and fine organization he can accomplish
much, but at all times he does need to exercise caution.

Rabbits seeking work or wanting to change their position

could be helped by contacting those in a position to give expert advice or who can assist them in some way. By taking positive action they could be given some information which will turn out to be of considerable value. In the last few months of the year these Rabbits will find much truth in the saying 'Nothing ventured, nothing gained.'

Financially, the latter part of the Rat year will be an expensive time and the Rabbit would do well to watch his general level of spending. However, he could be fortunate in the post-Christmas sales in acquiring some items that he has wanted for a long time and at most reasonable prices.

The Rabbit can also look forward to some pleasant times with his family and friends and some social events he attends early in December will prove especially enjoyable. Again, however, he should be wary about any rumours he might hear.

The Rabbit would also do well to use any spare time he has to attend to outstanding matters, particularly unfinished projects around the home or unanswered correspondence. He will find that with a concerted effort he will accomplish a great deal and this will leave him freer to enjoy the holiday period at the end of the year. After the activity of the Rat year, he deserves time to relax and enjoy himself – and enjoy himself he will!

The Year of the Ox starts on 7 February and will be a challenging but important year for the Rabbit. In 1997 he will find that some of his activities do not go as smoothly as he would like, but to compensate for this he will gain much valuable experience. Also, some of the events that occur will help him to reappraise his position and look at some of his longer term objectives. As a result, the Rabbit will be able to improve on some of his current ideas and also end up with a clearer idea of the direction he would like his life to take over the next few years.

As far as 1997 is concerned, however, in work matters this will be a demanding year and the Rabbit could find it difficult to achieve all he would like. Some of his plans may not meet with the response he had hoped and he could feel his efforts are passing unnoticed. Indeed, there will be times over the year when the Rabbit will feel frustrated and exasperated. However, while there will be testing moments for him, all the time he will be adding to his experience, winning the respect of others and learning more about his own capabilities. Out of the difficulties the Rabbit will face, he will gain much of value and become a stronger, wiser and certainly more resolute person. In future years he will be able to draw on what he has learned and it will serve him well as he starts to make further and more substantial progress.

To minimize the negative aspects that prevail in 1997 the Rabbit would do well to concentrate on specific matters, preferably in areas in which he has most experience. To try to achieve too much or be overly ambitious will lead to less satisfactory results as well as putting him under greater pressure. He should also be wary about starting ambitious new projects. If he bears these points in mind then the Rabbit can make a modest amount of progress and, while this might not always be as great as he would like, all the time he will be impressing others with his diligent and astute manner.

Rabbits seeking work or wanting to change their present duties should follow up any leads or advice they might have been given in the previous year as well as continue to stay alert for opportunities. Admittedly they may not always be successful in obtaining the exact position they desire, but they could find that a position they do attain will develop in a surprising manner and lead to some interesting openings in the future.

The Rabbit would also do well to take advantage of any opportunity to go on training courses or to consider undertaking some additional study, either at home or at an evening class. He could find that learning an additional skill will be a constructive use of his time as well as doing much to assist his future prospects. It is also a generally favourable year for those Rabbits in education and their progress and results will be worth all the time and effort they have devoted to their studies. Academically, what the Rabbit covers and achieves in the Ox year will prove significant in later years.

As far as financial matters are concerned, the Rabbit's skill in dealing with finance will prove useful. Throughout the year he would do well to keep a close watch on his level of spending and, if he enters into any large transaction, he should check the details closely. This is not a year in which the Rabbit can afford to take risks or become too complacent when dealing with finance. Provided he is his usual careful self he should incur few problems, but generally this is not a year for risks, speculation or being too extravagant in his spending.

The Rabbit is also one who prides himself on maintaining good relations with those around him and his tact and discreet manner will be a useful asset to him over the year. In 1997 he could find himself in a fraught situation and his calm and even-natured temperament will do much to defuse any awkwardness. Indeed, his poise and collected manner will impress others greatly over the year and this will help win him new friends and admirers.

In addition to the support his family gives him, the Rabbit can look forward to a most agreeable domestic life and will have every reason to feel satisfied with the achievements of those close to him. Also, if he intends to carry out any large projects around his home, he would do well to enlist the help of his family rather than tackle the jobs single-handed; he will find joint projects will not only prove satisfying for all concerned but also be quicker and easier to complete. Many Rabbits will get much pleasure from out-of-door activities in 1997 and for those who are keen gardeners, the year will prove most rewarding.

The Rabbit's social life will also contain some enjoyable moments, especially in the early summer months, and most Rabbits will have the opportunity to extend their circle of friends and acquaintances as the year progresses. Those who are unattached or seeking additional friends should make every effort to go out more and give themselves the opportunity to meet others. In all cases they will find that positive action on their part will bring pleasing results.

It is also important that the Rabbit does not neglect his own well-being during the year. He should make sure that he sets a regular time aside for his hobbies and recreational interests and, if he does not get much exercise during the day, should consider walking more or engaging in activities such as cycling or swimming. He will find this most beneficial for him.

Although the Rabbit may find it difficult to achieve as much as he would like over the year, what he does accomplish will certainly place him in good stead for the future. He will widen his experience and gain new friends as well as impress those with influence. While he may face problems and delays in carrying out some of his plans, the year will still contain some pleasant times and his domestic and social life in particular will bring give him considerable happiness.

As far as the different types of Rabbit are concerned, 1997 will be a mixed year for the *Metal Rabbit*. He is one who very much knows what he would like to achieve and has clear goals and aspirations. However, in 1997 he could find his progress slow and not all his plans may work out in the manner he would like. Some of 1997 could prove intensely frustrating. However, while there will be problems, the Metal Rabbit will comfortably surmount them and the year will still prove valuable for him. Over the year he will be given the chance to look closely at his future aims and reconsider some of his existing ideas. In some respects 1997 will be a year of re-evaluation and some of the new ideas that evolve will have an important bearing on the progress the Metal Rabbit will make over the next few years. However, when facing any obstacles in 1997, whether bureaucratic in nature or arising from those around him, he should look at the reason why they have occurred and see if he can work out an effective solution. By taking positive action, he will be able to prevent a re-occurrence of the problem as well as learn much in the process. In his work the Metal Rabbit will need to remain alert to all that is going on around him and be mindful of the views of his colleagues. He is by nature thorough and conscientious, but as far as possible he should avoid taking unnecessary risks or adopting too independent an attitude. Progress is possible in the Ox year but it will come through hard work and adapting to the conditions that prevail. As far as financial matters are concerned, the Metal Rabbit will need to keep a watchful eye on his level of spending. However, he could be delighted with some purchases that he makes for his accommodation, especially in the home furnishing line. Domestically, the year will be busy and eventful – at some times just a little too busy for his liking – but despite the demands on his time, his home life will bring him much pleasure. He should also listen closely to any advice that family members give him; while he may not fully agree with all they say, they do speak with his best interests at heart and there will be much wisdom in their words. The Metal Rabbit may not always have as much time for his hobbies as he would like but it would still be in his interests to set a regular time aside for them and give himself the chance to relax and unwind. To drive himself too hard – which could all be too tempting over the year – could leave him tired and listless and prone to minor ailments. In 1997 the Metal Rabbit does need to take good care of himself. He will also find any holidays or breaks he is able to take most beneficial for him. Although this may not be the easiest of years for the Metal Rabbit, providing he proceeds carefully and adapts to changing situations, he can do much to negate the more awkward aspects that prevail. Also, he will find that what he achieves over the year and the ideas he formulates will prove of great significance and help to him in the future.

There will have been times in recent years when the *Water Rabbit* may have felt that he has not been making as much use of his talents as he could. However, this will gradually change in 1997 and as far as the Water Rabbit's long-term fortunes are concerned, this will prove a significant year. During 1997 he will see several excellent opportunities to pursue, particularly in his work, and he should follow up any that interest him as well as promote any ideas he has. Admittedly the Water Rabbit's progress may not always be smooth or straightforward, but what he achieves will set in motion a sequence of events that will lead to even greater progress in future years. This is a year in which he will not only be sowing the seeds for his future but also beginning to reap the start of what will be a lengthy harvest! Throughout the year the Water Rabbit should, however, remain mindful of the views of those around him and alert to all that is happening. By keeping vigilant and well-informed he could learn of some information and opportunities that will be to his advantage. The period from September to November could prove significant for career matters. It is also a favourable year for the Water Rabbit to extend his skills and if there are any courses that interest him he would do well to follow these up. Financially, this will be a reasonable year for the Water Rabbit, although it would be in his interests to keep a watchful eye on his general level of spending. He is likely to spend a considerable amount on his home over the year and while he will not begrudge this – in fact he will be delighted with the acquisitions he makes and improvements he carries out – he must make sure he makes allowance for these in his budget. If not, and he stretches his resources too far, he could find he has to cut down substantially on his spending later in the year. The Water Rabbit's domestic life will be pleasurable but busy and throughout the year there will be many demands on his time. However, those around him will be a great source of pride to him and will also offer much useful advice and encouragement, particularly in times of uncertainty. Socially, too, the Water Rabbit can look forward to some pleasant times with his friends as well as to attending some interesting and sometimes prestigious functions. The Water Rabbit will also enjoy any holidays that he takes over the year, especially to destinations that he has not visited before. Generally, while 1997 will be a busy and active year for him, it will mark the start of a substantial upturn in his fortunes. The Water Rabbit has many skills and talents and over this year and next few years he will begin to realize his potential and make the progress he has been seeking for so long.

In some areas of his life 1997 will hold some memorable times for the *Wood Rabbit*, while in other areas he could face uncertainties and worries. Personally, however, this will be a splendid year – some Wood Rabbits will get married, see an addition to their family or achieve a long-held ambition. Those closest to them will be most supportive as well as provide much useful encouragement for their various activities. The Wood Rabbit's social life, too, will prove most enjoyable and he can look forward to many happy times with his friends. For those Wood Rabbits who are seeking friends or romance, the year will hold many excellent opportunities to meet others – particularly in the first few

months of the year – although they would do well to let
any new friendship develop gradually rather than rush into
any commitment. This way the friendship is more likely to
be based upon a securer foundation. Generally, however,
from a personal point of view, 1997 will prove a happy and
successful year. The Wood Rabbit should also listen carefully to any advice that he receives, particularly from those
who speak with experience. There will be much sound
advice in what they tell him and at all times the Wood
Rabbit would do well to remain mindful of the views and
feelings of those around him. He will also get much pleasure from his interests and hobbies over the year and
Wood Rabbits with creative aspirations would do well to
promote their skills. If they are able to get in contact with
those who share their interests they will find that this will
add considerably to their knowledge and enjoyment. The
Wood Rabbit may, however, find progress in his work more
difficult. There will be times when he will feel his efforts
are passing unnoticed and the results he desires are elusive.
However, while this may cause him to feel despondent, he
should not allow this to get the better of him. Throughout
the year he will be usefully adding to his experience and,
through his diligence and careful nature, earning the
respect of others. Also, he could be over-ambitious in his
expectations and trying to achieve results without having
the necessary experience behind him. This will be, as far as
his career aspirations are concerned, a year for learning,
with the positive results of his efforts becoming evident in
the next few years. Those Wood Rabbits seeking work
should persevere in their quest. While not all their
attempts will meet with success, many will attain a position

which will lead to greater opportunities in the future. The Wood Rabbit also needs to exercise care in financial matters, particularly as this is likely to be an expensive year for him. Ideally he should keep a close watch over all aspects of his expenditure and by putting his finances on a proper basis, he will find it easier to cope with his financial situation and avert possible problems later. However, while the Wood Rabbit will need to exercise care in both his work and financial activities, on a personal level the year will still hold some truly memorable times for him.

This will be a significant year for the *Fire Rabbit* with several important changes taking place. For the younger Fire Rabbit this could involve some changes in his education or, for the older Fire Rabbit, a move or having some improvements carried out on his accommodation. While the changes that do take place will prove unsettling and cause the Fire Rabbit some concern, the longer term results of what happens will work out in his favour. Some of the younger Fire Rabbits will change school or start a new range of subjects, either of which they could find daunting. However, they would do well to speak of any concerns they have to those around them and listen closely to what they are told. In many cases they could find that they are worrying unnecessarily, but the important thing is that they should not keep their worries to themselves. Those around them do want to help and by knowing of their anxieties will be better placed to assist. Those Fire Rabbits born in 1927 will also see several changes taking place and again if they have any concerns they should let them be known. Also, they should not allow themselves to be pressurized into making any decision against their better judgement. Admittedly there will be times in 1997 when they will be in a dilemma about what to do, especially over accommodation matters, but they should arrive at their decision in their own time and not take any action until they are satisfied it is the right course for them to take. Their family will prove most supportive to them over the year and they would do well to bear in mind the advice they give. Also, with the prospect of moving or having alterations carried out, the Fire Rabbit should be careful if he attempts to move heavy items. Without care he could sprain himself and cause himself some discomfort. Again those around will be pleased to help, should he ask. However, while this will be a year of change for many Fire Rabbits, it will still contain many enjoyable times. In particular the Fire Rabbit will delight in the travelling that he undertakes and should take advantage of any opportunities to meet up with friends or relations he has not seen for some time. Such a meeting will give all concerned much pleasure. His hobbies, too, will provide him with some absorbing times and he should consider making contact with others who share his interests. He will find this will not only add to his enjoyment and knowledge, but will also lead to several new friendships. Creative pursuits in particular are likely to go well and the Fire Rabbit will also take much delight in gardening and other outdoor activities he engages in. Although the year will contain some times of uncertainty and concern, generally there will be much that the Fire Rabbit will enjoy and his domestic and social life, together with his interests, will provide him with much pleasure.

This will be a reasonable year for the *Earth Rabbit* and

while not all his activities may go as smoothly as he would like, he will be generally content with his level of progress. In much of what he does, he tends to be thorough and careful, and such an attitude will serve him well during the year. In his work his conscientious manner will impress and many Earth Rabbits will be given additional responsibilities as the year progresses. However, when taking these on, the Earth Rabbit should make sure he knows what is expected of him and should he have any query or doubts over any employment matter he would do well to check. This way future misunderstandings could be avoided. The Earth Rabbit also needs to exercise care when completing any important forms or documents and similarly, if he enters into a large financial transaction, he does need to read the small print closely. If he is to avoid problems, matters involving paperwork do need careful handling. The Earth Rabbit would, however, do well to give some thought to his longer term future over the year and discuss his thoughts with those around him. Some of the ideas he has will prove important over the next few years, but as far as 1997 is concerned, he should avoid taking any precipitous action. Time is on his side and he should not allow himself to be rushed into taking any major decision until he is fully satisfied it is the right one. His domestic life will be generally busy and many Earth Rabbits will have good reason to be involved in a family celebration over the year; possibly the birth of a grandchild or the splendid achievement of someone close. However, while domestically the year will go well, the Earth Rabbit does need to be mindful of the views and interests of those around him and avoid the all too easy temptation of becoming so involved in his own concerns that he does not pay as much attention to others as he should. If he is not careful, this could result in some tensions. The Earth Rabbit will greatly enjoy any holidays or breaks he takes and will find out-of-door activities especially satisfying. For those Earth Rabbits who enjoy gardening, walking, following sport or exploring the countryside, the year will contain many pleasurable moments. With care, 1997 will prove a satisfying and fulfilling year for the Earth Rabbit.

FAMOUS RABBITS

Paula Abdul, Prince Albert, Rob Andrew, Cecil Beaton, Harry Belafonte, Ingrid Bergman, Melvyn Bragg, Gordon Brown, James Caan, Nicholas Cage, Thomas Carlyle, Lewis Carroll, Fidel Castro, John Cleese, Confucius, Christopher Cross, Dr Jack Cunningham, Marie Curie, Kenny Dalglish, Peter Davison, Johnny Depp, Albert Einstein, George Eliot, Peter Falk, W. C. Fields, Peter Fonda, Jodie Foster, James Fox, Sir David Frost, James Galway, Cary Grant, Edvard Grieg, John Gummer, Oliver Hardy, Seamus Heaney, Paul Hogan, Bob Hope, Whitney Houston, John Hurt, Chrissie Hynde, Clive James, Henry James, David Jason, Anatoli Karpov, Gary Kasparov, Michael Keaton, John Keats, Judith Krantz, Danny La Rue, Cheryl Ladd, Julian Lennon, Patrick Lichfield, Gina Lollobrigida, Robert Ludlum, Ali MacGraw, Trevor McDonald, George Michael, Arthur Miller, Colin Montgomerie, Roger Moore, James Naughtie, Nanette Newman, Brigitte Nielsen, Tatum O'Neal, Christina Onassis, George Orwell, John Peel, Eva Peron, William Perry, Edith Piaf, Chris Rea, John Redwood, John Ruskin, Ken Russell, Mort Sahl, Elisabeth Schwarzkopf, George C. Scott, Selina Scott, Sir Walter Scott, Neil Sedaka, Jane Seymour, Gillian Shephard, Georges Simenon, Neil Simon, Frank Sinatra, Dusty Springfield, Sting, Jimmy Tarbuck, Sir Denis Thatcher, J. R. R. Tolkien, Arturo Toscanini, Tina Turner, Luther Vandross, Queen Victoria, Terry Waite, Andy Warhol, Orson Welles, Walt Whitman, Yazz.

16 FEBRUARY 1904 ∼ 3 FEBRUARY 1905   *Wood Dragon*

3 FEBRUARY 1916 ∼ 22 JANUARY 1917   *Fire Dragon*

23 JANUARY 1928 ∼ 9 FEBRUARY 1929   *Earth Dragon*

8 FEBRUARY 1940 ∼ 26 JANUARY 1941   *Metal Dragon*

27 JANUARY 1952 ∼ 13 FEBRUARY 1953   *Water Dragon*

13 FEBRUARY 1964 ∼ 1 FEBRUARY 1965   *Wood Dragon*

31 JANUARY 1976 ∼ 17 FEBRUARY 1977   *Fire Dragon*

17 FEBRUARY 1988 ∼ 5 FEBRUARY 1989   *Earth Dragon*

THE
DRAGON

THE PERSONALITY OF THE DRAGON

Always bear in mind that your own resolution to succeed
is more important than any other one thing.
   – Abraham Lincoln: a Dragon

The Dragon is born under the sign of luck. He is a proud
and lively character and has a tremendous amount of self-
confidence. He is also highly intelligent and very quick to
take advantage of any opportunities that occur. He is ambitious and determined and will do well in practically
anything which he attempts. He is also something of a
perfectionist and will always try and maintain the high
standards he sets himself.

The Dragon does not suffer fools gladly and will be
quick to criticize anyone or anything that displeases him.
He can be blunt and forthright in his views and is certainly
not renowned for being either tactful or diplomatic. He
does, however, often take people at their word and can
occasionally be rather gullible. If he ever feels that his trust
has been abused or his dignity wounded he can sometimes
become very bitter and it will take him a long time to
forgive and forget.

The Dragon is usually very outgoing and is particularly
adept at attracting attention and publicity. He enjoys being
in the limelight and is often at his best when he is
confronted by a difficult problem or tense situation. In
some respects he is a showman and he rarely lacks an audi-
ence. His views and opinions are very highly valued and he
invariably has something interesting – and sometimes

controversial – to say.

He has considerable energy and is often prepared to work long and unsocial hours in order to achieve what he wants. He can, however, be rather impulsive and does not always consider the consequences of his actions. He also has a tendency to live for the moment and there is nothing that riles him more than to be kept waiting. The Dragon hates delay and can get extremely impatient and irritable over even the smallest of hold-ups.

The Dragon has an enormous faith in his abilities, but he does run the risk of becoming over-confident and unless he is careful he can sometimes make grave errors of judgement. While this may prove disastrous at the time, he does have the tenacity and ability to bounce back and pick up the pieces again.

The Dragon has such an assertive personality, so much will-power and such a desire to succeed that he will often reach the top of his chosen profession. He has considerable leadership qualities and will do well in positions where he can put his own ideas and policies into practice. He is usually successful in politics, show business, as the manager of his own department or business, and in any job which brings him into contact with the media.

The Dragon relies a tremendous amount on his own judgement and can be scornful of other people's advice. He likes to feel self-sufficient and there are many Dragons who cherish their independence to such a degree that they prefer to remain single throughout their lives. However, the Dragon will often have numerous admirers and there are many who are attracted by his flamboyant personality and striking looks. If he does marry, he will usually marry young and will find himself particularly well-suited to those born under the signs of the Snake, Rat, Monkey and Rooster. He will also find that the Rabbit, Pig, Horse and Goat make ideal companions and will readily join in with many of his escapades. Two Dragons will also get on well together, as they understand each other, but the Dragon may not find things so easy with the Ox and Dog, as both will be critical of his impulsive and somewhat extrovert manner. He will also find it difficult to form an alliance with the Tiger, for the Tiger, like the Dragon, tends to speak his mind, is very strong-willed and likes to take the lead.

The female Dragon knows what she wants in life and sets about everything she does in a very determined and positive manner. No job is too small for her and she is often prepared to work extremely hard until she has secured her objective. She is immensely practical and somewhat liberated. She hates being bound by routine and petty restrictions and likes to have sufficient freedom to be able to go off and do what she wants to do. She will keep her house tidy but is not one for spending hours on house-work – there are far too many other things that she feels are more important and that she prefers to do. Like her male counterpart, she has a tendency to speak her mind.

The Dragon usually has many interests and enjoys sport and other outdoor activities. He also likes to travel and often prefers to visit places that are off the beaten track rather than head for popular tourist attractions. He has a very adventurous streak in him and providing his financial circumstances permit – and the Dragon is usually sensible with his money – he will travel considerable distances during his lifetime.

The Dragon is a very flamboyant character and while he can be demanding of others and in his early years rather precocious, he will have many friends and will nearly always be the centre of attention. He has charisma and so much confidence in himself that he can often become a source of inspiration for others. In China he is the leader of the carnival and he is also blessed with an inordinate share of luck.

THE FIVE DIFFERENT TYPES OF DRAGON

In addition to the 12 signs of the Chinese zodiac, there are five elements and these have a strengthening or moderating influence on the sign. The effects of the five elements on the Dragon are described below, together with the years in which the elements were exercising their influence. Therefore all Dragons born in 1940 are Metal Dragons, those born in 1952 are Water Dragons, and so on.

Metal Dragon: 1940
This Dragon is very strong-willed and has a particularly forceful personality. He is energetic, ambitious and tries to be scrupulous in his dealings with others. He can also be blunt and to the point and usually has no hesitation in

speaking his mind. If people disagree with him, or are not prepared to co-operate, he is more than happy to go his own way. The Metal Dragon usually has very high moral values and is held in great esteem by his friends and colleagues.

Water Dragon: 1952

This Dragon is friendly, easy-going and intelligent. He is quick-witted and rarely lets an opportunity slip by. However, he is not as impatient as some of the other types of Dragon and is more prepared to wait for results rather than expect everything to happen that moment. He has an understanding nature and is prepared to share his ideas and co-operate with others. His main failing, though, is a tendency to jump from one thing to another rather than concentrate on the job in hand. He has a good sense of humour and is an effective speaker.

Wood Dragon: 1904, 1964

The Wood Dragon is practical, imaginative and inquisitive. He loves delving into all manner of subjects and can quite often come up with some highly original ideas. He is a thinker and a doer and has sufficient drive and commit-ment to put many of his ideas into practice. He is more diplomatic than some of the other types of Dragon and has a good sense of humour. He is very astute in business matters and can also be most generous.

Fire Dragon: 1916, 1976

This Dragon is ambitious, articulate and has a tremendous desire to succeed. He is a hard and conscientious worker and is often admired for his integrity and forthright nature. He is very strong-willed and has considerable leadership qualities. He can, however, rely a bit too much on his own judgement and fail to take into account the views and feelings of others. He can also be rather aloof and it would certainly be in his own interests to let others join in more with his various activities. The Fire Dragon usually gets much enjoyment from music, literature and the arts.

Earth Dragon: 1928, 1988

The Earth Dragon tends to be quieter and more reflective than some of the other types of Dragon. He has a wide variety of interests and is keenly aware of what is going on around him. He also has clear objectives and usually has no problems in obtaining support and backing for any of his ventures. He is very astute in financial matters and is often able to accumulate considerable wealth. He is a good organizer, although he can at times be rather bureaucratic and fussy. He mixes well with others and has a large circle of friends.

PROSPECTS FOR THE DRAGON
IN 1997

The Chinese New Year starts on 7 February 1997. Until then, the old year, the Year of the Rat, is still making its presence felt.

The Year of the Rat (19 February 1996 to 6 February 1997) is a highly favourable year for the Dragon and in what remains of it he can accomplish much. He should use any opportunity he gets to further his ideas and should also pursue any openings he sees. With a positive attitude and determined approach, the Dragon's activities can meet with a good level of success. Those around him will also prove most co-operative and the Dragon should experience few problems in winning the support of others.

Many Dragons will have made substantial progress in their work over the year and the favourable aspects for employment matters will continue to the end of the Rat year. In view of this, all Dragons should make a concerted effort to promote themselves and their skills at this time; indeed, the bold and assertive Dragon can make considerable headway in the last few months of the year. Also, those Dragons seeking work or wanting to change their position should remain active in following up any opportunities they see. The months of October, December and January all bode well and many Dragons could see interesting developments in their work at this time.

The Dragon will also have fared well in financial matters throughout the Rat year and while the closing months will tend to be an expensive time, provided he remains sensible in his level of spending, he will end the year in a much improved financial position than at the start.

The Dragon's domestic and social life will also have gone well and again, the last few months of the Rat year will prove an enjoyable time. The Dragon can look forward to attending several pleasant social functions as the year draws to a close and at one of these he could meet someone or learn of some information, either of which could prove significant over the next 12 months.

For Dragons seeking romance or new friendships, the closing stages of the Rat year can prove a favourable time. These Dragons should make every effort to go out more and to places where they are likely to meet others. The Rat year does favour romance and the making of new friendships and, by taking positive action, the lonely or unattached Dragon can do much to improve his social life.

Generally, the Rat year is a most encouraging time for the Dragon and provided he sets about his activities in his usual ebullient manner he can and will achieve much.

The Year of the Ox starts on 7 February and will be a variable year for the Dragon. Over the year he will need to restrain his rather impulsive nature and exercise caution in his various undertakings. This is not a year in which he can afford to take risks or adopt too independent an attitude. The Dragon, for all his admirable qualities, does like to be his own master and have his own way but in the Ox year this will not always be possible.

However, while the Ox year will have an inhibiting effect upon the Dragon, this need not be an adverse time. Some areas of his life will proceed smoothly and, with care, the Dragon could end the year with some worthy gains to his credit.

In his work the Dragon can make a modest amount of progress, although he needs to be realistic in his expectations. To try to be over-ambitious or take on too many activities all at the same time will only lead to disappointment. Also, rather than spread his energies too widely, the Dragon will find the best results will come from concentrating on specific matters and areas in which he is most experienced. He should also be wary about embarking on any new and risky ventures. This is a year when the Dragon needs to be cautious in his work as well as keep alert to all that is happening around him. To ignore the views of his colleagues or not adapt to new situations could undermine his level of progress. True, the Dragon may have set ideas on what he wants to achieve, but this is just not a year in which he can go it alone or isolate himself too much from the events going on around him. Providing he heeds this advice and continues to work to the best of his abilities (and the Ox year does favour and reward the industrious!), then the Dragon will find his progress a little easier.

Dragons who are wanting to change their position or seeking work should, however, remain vigilant throughout the year. While not all their applications may meet with success, they could be successful in obtaining a position which will not only usefully add to their experience but develop in an interesting manner over the next few years. The months of March, September and October could all prove important for employment matters.

This is also an excellent year for the Dragon to further

his skills and if there are any subjects or training courses that interest him, he should investigate further. What the Dragon learns in 1997 will be of considerable value in later years. Similarly, those Dragons in education will make good headway over the year and any qualifications or expertise that they can obtain will do much to enhance their prospects.

The Dragon does, however, need to be careful when dealing with financial matters. This is not a year when he can take risks and he should be wary of any highly speculative ventures or 'get rich quick' schemes that he may hear about. He would also do well to keep a watchful eye on his level of expenditure and while he may face some expenses over the year, particularly involving travel and his accommodation, he should make sure he makes allowances for them in his budget. With care and a certain restraint, the Dragon can avoid running into financial problems, but if he takes risks or is too complacent in his financial dealings, then he could find he is having to dig deep into his savings. These may not be as easy to replenish as he first thought!

Domestically, the Ox year will be an active year for the Dragon, particularly as many Dragons will devote much of their spare time to carrying out improvements to their accommodation and garden. Although this work, and general DIY activities, will prove time-consuming, the Dragon will be delighted with the finished result. His family will be most supportive over the year and happy to lend him assistance and advice whenever required. The Dragon can also look forward to some memorable family occasions in 1997 and he will find family outings, particularly those arranged on the spur of the moment, especially pleasing.

Travel is generally well aspected in 1997 and all Dragons should try to go away at least once over the year. They will find a change of scene and the break it gives them most beneficial.

The Dragon's social life will also prove enjoyable and any romance or new friendship that the Dragon started in the Rat year is likely to blossom. For those Dragons who are either lonely or unattached, there will be several excellent opportunities to meet others, especially in the early summer months. On a personal level, both domestically and socially, the Ox year can bring the Dragon much happiness, but a word of warning: the Dragon does tend to have a domineering nature and can sometimes, however unwittingly, impose his ideas and views on others. To be too demanding or inconsiderate of others could lead to tensions and it is a point the Dragon does need to watch. Similarly, if he finds himself in a fraught or difficult situation, the Dragon should remain tactful and discreet. To speak too candidly or lose his temper could result in him saying things he will later regret and will undermine the normally good relations he enjoys with those around him. As with so many areas of his life, in the Ox year the Dragon needs to be careful and exercise some restraint over his sometimes over-zealous nature.

Although there will be many demands on the Dragon's time in 1997, he should still make sure that he sets a regular time aside for his own personal interests. He could find out-of-door activities most satisfying and with this being a favoured year for travel, he will enjoy the journeys and holidays he is able to take. Also, if he does not get much

exercise during the day, he could find some additional physical activity will do much to help his general level of fitness.
Those Dragons who take part in or follow sport can also
look forward to some gratifying times over the year.

While the Dragon's general level of progress may not
always be as great as he would like, provided he is careful
in his activities and remains mindful of all that is going on
around him, this can still be a reasonable year for him. In
particular, the experience he gains and skills he is able to
acquire will prove of considerable value to him over the
next few years. In this respect, the Ox year can be viewed
as an important and constructive one for him. In addition,
his family, friends and various interests will also bring him
much happiness and satisfaction over the year.

As far as the different types of Dragon are concerned, this
will be an interesting year for the *Metal Dragon*. There
will be several opportunities for him to improve upon his
present position, particularly in his work, and he should
stay alert for ways in which he can promote his talents.
With good timing and by taking into account the conditions that prevail, the Metal Dragon can make reasonable
progress. Also many Metal Dragons will take much delight
in the completion of a project they have been engaged on
for some time and which will bring them some well
deserved credit. However, in spite of this, the Metal
Dragon should avoid taking undue risks or acting without
the support of others. Admittedly he may hold very set
ideas on what he wants to achieve, but if he is to make any
sort of progress he does need to tread carefully and act in
close co-operation with others. This is just not a year when

he can push his luck too far or maintain too independent an attitude. The Metal Dragon would also do well to give some thought to his long-term future over the year. In this he should discuss any ideas he has with those close to him but should not be in a hurry to commit himself to any major decision just yet. Time is on his side and he should regard 1997 more as a year for making and deciding upon future plans than for taking action. He will also need to exercise care in financial matters and should avoid risky undertakings or spending too much without regard to his current situation. This is not a year he can be too complacent or overly indulgent with his finances. More positively, however, the Metal Dragon's domestic and social life will bring him much pleasure. He will delight in the activities of those around him, especially in the success enjoyed by someone younger than himself. There will also be good cause for a family celebration over the year. The Metal Dragon's hobbies and interests, too, will go well and will provide him with many absorbing hours. Some Metal Dragons could also find that a hobby of theirs or skill they have recently taught themselves could prove lucrative or develop in a most unexpected manner. If the Metal Dragon does have any creative talents or aspirations, this would be a good year to bring his work to the attention of others. The travelling he undertakes will also go well and he will find any holidays and breaks he takes most beneficial. Generally, if the Metal Dragon sets about his activities with care, avoids being unduly stubborn over any matter (thereby causing friction between himself and others) and remains mindful of the conditions that prevail, this will be a reasonable and constructive year for him. The thoughts he gives to his future will also prove most helpful to him over the next few years.

The Year of the Ox will be quite an active year for the *Water Dragon* and while he may not always be able to make the progress he would like, this will still be a satisfying year for him. To get the best results, however, he needs to concentrate on areas that he is most familiar with rather than embarking on ambitious new ventures. Ideally he should consolidate any recent gains he has made and continue to set about his activities in his usual thorough way. This is more a year for taking stock of his present position and adding to his experience than for making swift progress. However, if there are any courses that the Water Dragon can take, whether in work or seeking work, he should follow these up. Any additional training will not only be a productive use of his time but also do much to enhance his longer term prospects. Also, the acquisition of a new skill will prove a stimulating challenge for the Water Dragon and provide him with a new incentive to make the most of himself and his abilities. The results of his efforts will be rewarded in the closing stages of the Ox year, with the months from September to December being a favoured time. Throughout the year, however, the Water Dragon does need to adapt to any new situations that occur in his work and also remain keenly aware of the views of his colleagues. He is usually most considerate, but 1997 is not a year when he can afford to be too independent in his actions or views. Financial matters will go reasonably well for the Water Dragon, although he could have several large expenses to meet, especially connected with transport and his accommodation. When large expenses do arise he should make sure he makes allowances for these in his budget. In this it would be useful if he were to carry out a thorough review of his financial situation and cut down on any expenses that are no longer necessary or essential. He could be pleasantly surprised at the difference this could make. The Water Dragon's domestic life will be generally busy over the year and there will be times when he will despair of all he has to do, particularly in the way of household and maintenance jobs. However, those around him will be most supportive and the Water Dragon should not hesitate to ask for assistance at busy times. His family will also be a source of much pride to him and he can look forward to some truly memorable times with both family members and close friends. It is also important that the Water Dragon does not neglect himself or his own interests over the year. His interests do provide him with an excellent opportunity to rest and unwind and give him a much needed break from his everyday concerns. Also, with travel being well aspected, he should make sure he goes away for a holiday or several breaks over the year. He will find them of much benefit. Although this will be a busy year for the Water Dragon and his progress may not always be as great as he would like, with care and his usual good sense, this will still be a pleasant year for him. What he learns and achieves now will hold him in excellent stead for the progress he will make in future years.

This will be an interesting year for the *Wood Dragon* and while his level of progress may not be all that he had hoped, what he does achieve will prove significant. Throughout the year he will be usefully adding to his experience and some of the events that occur will cause him to modify some of his existing plans and objectives. In many cases, the new ideas that he formulates will be superior to his existing ones and will help give him a clearer idea of where he should now be channelling his energies. In many respects, the Ox year will prove an important and constructive year for him. In his work, however, the Wood Dragon should be prepared to adapt to any new situations that arise and keep himself informed on all that is going on around him. He should also take advantage of any opportunity to extend his experience and skills – again, what he learns over the year will prove of significance later. Those Dragons seeking work should actively follow up any openings that they see but should also be adventurous in some of the positions that they try for. Some could be successful in obtaining a completely different position from anything they have done before and, while this might not be what they originally intended, it will reveal talents they never knew they possessed and lead to further opportunities in the future. For many Wood Dragons, the experience that they gain over the year will do much to enhance their future prospects. The Wood Dragon will fare reasonably well in financial matters, although it would be in his interests to keep a close watch over his level of spending. If he intends to make any large purchase over the year he would do well to compare prices in different outlets rather than rush into a transaction – this way he could make considerable savings. The Wood Dragon's family life will be busy and at times demanding but it will also be highly pleasurable. He can look forward to having some enjoyable times with those around him, although he should be prepared to discuss his ideas and any concerns he might have with family members rather than keep them to himself. They do have his best interests at heart and will give him much useful advice. The travelling that the Wood Dragon undertakes over the year will also go well and he will thoroughly enjoy any holidays that he is able to take, especially to destinations that are both new to him and in some ways unusual. Although his progress during the year may not be as great as he would like, there will still be many memorable times for him; most significantly, the experience he gets and ideas he formulates will prove of considerable value to him in the future, probably more so than he may realize at the time. For some Wood Dragons the Year of the Ox will mark the first stages of a new and more positive phase in their life.

This is a year of much potential for the *Fire Dragon* but just how much he achieves and how he enjoys the year is heavily dependent upon him. The Fire Dragon has many fine gifts and talents but he does tend to be impatient for results and can sometimes be impulsive in his actions. In 1997 he needs to plan his activities carefully, set himself clear objectives and at all times remain mindful of the views and feelings of others. Although he may be sure in his own mind what he wishes to attain, he must be prepared to accept existing situations, not take undue risks or adopt a go it alone attitude. Provided he heeds this advice he can make steady progress over the year and gain much useful experience as well as impress others, all of which will greatly assist his future prospects. In his work he should continue to set about his duties in his usual diligent manner but also seek out opportunities which will add to his skills. Indeed, all Fire Dragons, whether in work or seeking work, would do well to go on any courses they might be eligible for and if they are able to extend their qualifications they will find this will be of considerable benefit to them in future years. Work matters may not always go entirely smoothly in 1997 but it will be a most constructive year for the Fire Dragon and will help pave the way for the significant advances he will make over the next few years. His personal life will bring him much happiness over the year and many Fire Dragons will have good reason for a personal celebration, either by getting engaged or married or seeing an addition to their family. However, while there will be times of much joy in 1997, the Fire Dragon does need to remain considerate of others and cannot expect to have things always his own way. He must accept that some may not share his views or be as enthusiastic over certain projects as he is and he should also accept any criticism or advice he receives in the spirit it is given: constructively. With the right attitude the Fire Dragon will learn much of value over the year. He will, however, need to watch his financial situation carefully and should he enter into any large transaction, make sure he is fully conversant with any terms he is placed under. As far as financial matters are concerned, this is a year for care and prudence. Generally, though, this will be a pleasing year for the Fire Dragon and one in which he will gain much valuable experience. Personally, too, the year will contain many splendid times for him.

This will be a generally satisfying year for the *Earth Dragon*. In particular his various interests and hobbies will bring him much pleasure, especially those that take him out of doors or allow him to meet with others. Indeed, one of his interests could develop in quite an unexpected way and he would do well to promote his knowledge and any special skills he has, perhaps by writing about them in a specialist publication. He could find his talents much in demand during the year! The Earth Dragon can also look forward to some memorable times with his family and friends and a younger relation in particular will be a great source of pride to him. Any additional support and advice he feels able to give will be much valued. However, while on a personal level the year will be pleasing, there will be some matters which will give him cause for concern. These are more likely to be niggling than serious and could involve complications over a bureaucratic matter or a transaction he is trying to carry out. In dealing with any problems that do arise, the Earth Dragon would do well to seek the advice of others rather than keep the worry to himself. He will find those around him are most support-ive and will help ease any concern that he might have. Throughout the year the Earth Dragon will find much truth in the saying 'A worry shared is a worry halved.' Similarly, those Earth Dragons involved in education could at times feel daunted by what is being asked of them; again, they would be helped if they were to speak to others about their concern rather than keep it to themselves. Generally, despite any initial misgivings that the young Earth Dragon might have about school or new subjects he takes up, he will find that events will move in his favour and his worries are usually unfounded. However, while most Earth Dragons will face some uncertainties over the year, these need not mar the generally pleasant times that the year holds for them. The Earth Dragon will also enjoy the travelling that he undertakes and will take much delight in any holidays or breaks. He could find outings to local places of interest especially enjoyable. Overall, this will be a pleasing year for the Earth Dragon but he should remember that at times of uncertainty it really would be in his interests to speak to others rather than shoulder the problem single-handed. This way he could save himself a lot of often needless worry.

FAMOUS DRAGONS

Jeffrey Archer, Roseanne Arnold, Joan Baez, Michael Barrymore, Count Basie, Bill Beaumont, St Bernadette, George Bernard Shaw, James Brown, Neneh Cherry, Julie Christie, Kenneth Clarke, James Coburn, Ben Crenshaw, Bing Crosby, Roald Dahl, Salvador Dali, Charles Darwin, Susan Dey, Neil Diamond, Bo Diddley, Matt Dillon, Christian Dior, Frank Dobson, Placido Domingo, Fats Domino, Stephen Dorrell, Faye Dunaway, Prince Edward, Adam Faith, Bruce Forsyth, Sigmund Freud, Michael Gambon, James Garner, Sir John Gielgud, Graham Greene, Che Guevara, David Hasselhoff, Sir Edward Heath, Johnny Herbert, Joan of Arc, Tom Jones, Imran Khan, Martin Luther King, Eartha Kitt, Ian Lang, John Lennon, Abraham Lincoln, Lee Majors, Queen Margrethe II of Denmark, Brian Mawhinny, Yehudi Menuhin, François Mitterrand, Bob Monkhouse, Hosni Mubarak, Florence Nightingale, Nick Nolte, Al Pacino, Elaine Paige, Gregory Peck, Sir Cliff Richard, Mel Smith, Ringo Starr, Princess Stephanie of Monaco, Shirley Temple, Raquel Welch, Mae West.

4 FEBRUARY 1905 ⁓ 24 JANUARY 1906		*Wood Snake*
23 JANUARY 1917 ⁓ 10 FEBRUARY 1918		*Fire Snake*
10 FEBRUARY 1929 ⁓ 29 JANUARY 1930		*Earth Snake*
27 JANUARY 1941 ⁓ 14 FEBRUARY 1942		*Metal Snake*
14 FEBRUARY 1953 ⁓ 2 FEBRUARY 1954		*Water Snake*
2 FEBRUARY 1965 ⁓ 20 JANUARY 1966		*Wood Snake*
18 FEBRUARY 1977 ⁓ 6 FEBRUARY 1978		*Fire Snake*
6 FEBRUARY 1989 ⁓ 26 JANUARY 1990		*Earth Snake*

THE
SNAKE

THE PERSONALITY OF THE SNAKE

The right man is the one that seizes the moment.
— *Johann Wolfgang von Goethe: a Snake*

The Snake is born under the sign of wisdom. He is highly intelligent and his mind is forever active. He is always planning and always looking for ways in which he can use his considerable skills. He is a deep thinker and likes to meditate and reflect.

Many times during his life he will shed one of his famous Snake skins and take up new interests or start a completely different job. The Snake enjoys a challenge and he rarely makes mistakes. He is a skilful organizer, has considerable business acumen and is usually lucky in money matters. Most Snakes are financially secure in their later years, provided they do not gamble – the Snake has the distinction of being the worst gambler in the whole of the Chinese zodiac!

The Snake generally has a calm and placid nature and prefers the quieter things in life. He does not like to be in a frenzied atmosphere and hates being hurried into making a quick decision. He also does not like interference in his affairs and tends to rely on his own judgement rather than listen to advice.

The Snake can at times appear solitary. He is quiet, reserved and sometimes has difficulty in communicating with others. He has little time for idle gossip and will certainly not suffer fools gladly. He does, however, have a good sense of humour and this is particularly appreciated in times of crisis.

The Snake is certainly not afraid of hard work and is thorough in all that he does. He is very determined and can occasionally be ruthless in order to achieve his aims. His confidence, will-power and quick thinking usually ensure his success, but should he fail it will often take a long time for him to recover. He cannot bear failure and is a very bad loser.

The Snake can also be evasive and does not willingly let people into his confidence. This secrecy and distrust can sometimes work against him and it is a trait which all Snakes should try to overcome.

Another characteristic of the Snake is his tendency to rest after any sudden or prolonged bout of activity. He burns up so much nervous energy that without proper care he can – if he is not careful – be susceptible to high blood pressure and nervous disorders.

It has sometimes been said that the Snake is a late starter in life and this is mainly because it often takes him a while to find a job with which he is genuinely happy. However, the Snake will usually do well in any position which involves research and writing and where he is given sufficient freedom to develop his own ideas and plans. He makes a good teacher, politician, personnel manager and social adviser.

The Snake chooses his friends carefully and, while he keeps a tight control over his finances, he can be particularly generous to those he likes. He will think nothing of buying expensive gifts or treating his friends or loved ones to the best theatre seats in town. In return he demands loyalty. The Snake is very possessive and he can become extremely jealous and hurt if he finds his trust has been abused.

The Snake is also renowned for his good looks and is never short of admirers. The female Snake in particular is most alluring. She has style, grace and excellent (and usually expensive) taste in clothes. A keen socializer, she is likely to have a wide range of friends and has a happy knack of impressing those who matter. She has numerous interests and her advice and opinions are often highly valued. She is generally a calm-natured person and while she involves herself in many activities, she likes to retain a certain amount of privacy in her undertakings.

The affairs of the heart are very important to the Snake and he will often have many romances before he finally settles down. He will find that he is particularly well suited to those born under the signs of the Ox, Dragon, Rabbit and Rooster. Provided he is allowed sufficient freedom to pursue his own interests, he can also build up a very satis-factory relationship with the Rat, Horse, Goat, Monkey and Dog, but he should try to steer clear of another Snake as they could very easily become jealous of each other. The Snake will also have difficulty in getting on with the honest and down-to-earth Pig, and will find the Tiger far too much of a disruptive influence on his quiet and peace-loving ways.

The Snake certainly appreciates the finer things in life. He enjoys good food and often takes a keen interest in the arts. He also enjoys reading and is invariably drawn to subjects such as philosophy, political thought, religion or the occult. He is fascinated by the unknown and his enquiring mind is always looking for answers. Some of the world's most original thinkers have been Snakes, and – although he may not readily admit it – the Snake is often psychic and relies a lot on intuition.

The Snake is certainly not the most energetic member of the Chinese zodiac. He prefers to proceed at his own pace and to do the things he wants. He is very much his own master and throughout his life he will try his hand at many things. He is something of a dabbler, but at some time – usually when he least expects it – his hard work and efforts will be recognized and he will invariably meet with the success and the financial security which he so much desires.

THE FIVE DIFFERENT TYPES OF SNAKE

In addition to the 12 signs of the Chinese zodiac, there are five elements and these have a strengthening or moderating influence on the sign. The effects of the five elements on the Snake are described below, together with the years in which the elements were exercising their influence. Therefore all Snakes born in 1941 are Metal Snakes, those born in 1953 are Water Snakes, and so on.

Metal Snake: 1941

This Snake is quiet, confident and fiercely independent. He often prefers to work on his own and will only let a privileged few into his confidence. He is quick to spot opportunities and will set about achieving his objectives with an awesome determination. He is astute in financial matters and will often invest his money well. He also has a liking for the finer things in life and has a good appreciation of the arts, literature, music and good food. He usually has a small group of extremely good friends and can be generous to his loved ones.

Water Snake: 1953

This Snake has a wide variety of interests. He enjoys studying all manner of subjects and is capable of undertaking quite detailed research and becoming a specialist in his chosen area. He is highly intelligent, has a good memory, and is particularly astute when dealing with business and financial matters. He tends to be quietly spoken and a little reserved, but he does have sufficient strength of character to make his views known and attain his ambitions. He is very loyal to his family and friends.

Wood Snake: 1905, 1965

The Wood Snake has a friendly temperament and a good understanding of human nature. He is able to communicate well with others and often has many friends and admirers. He is witty, intelligent and ambitious. He has numerous interests and prefers to live in a quiet, stable environment where he can work without too much interference. He enjoys the arts and usually derives much pleasure from collecting paintings and antiques. His advice is often very highly valued, particularly on social and domestic matters.

Fire Snake: 1917, 1977

The Fire Snake tends to be more forceful, outgoing and energetic than some of the other types of Snake. He is ambitious, confident and never slow in voicing his opinions – and he can be very abrasive to those he does not like. He does, however, have many leadership qualities and can win the respect and support of many with his firm and resolute manner. He usually has a good sense of humour, a wide circle of friends and a very active social life. The Fire Snake is also a keen traveller.

Earth Snake: 1929, 1989

The Earth Snake is charming, amusing and has a very amiable manner. He is conscientious and reliable in his work and approaches everything he does in a level-headed and sensible way. He can, however, tend to err on the cautious side and never likes to be hassled into making a decision. He is extremely adept in dealing with financial matters and is a shrewd investor. He has many friends and is very supportive towards the members of his family.

PROSPECTS FOR THE SNAKE
IN 1997

The Chinese New Year starts on 7 February 1997. Until then, the old year, the Year of the Rat, is still making its presence felt.

The Year of the Rat (19 February 1996 to 6 February 1997) will have been an eventful year for the Snake and in what remains of it he can accomplish much. Rat years very much favour innovation and the Snake, with his alert and creative mind, is well placed to take advantage of this trend. In the remaining months of the Rat year the Snake should promote himself and his ideas as much as he can. Admittedly, the Snake may not be the most assertive of signs, but to take advantage of the progressive trends he really should make the effort. The period from late October 1996 to January 1997 could prove highly import-ant for him, especially as far as work matters and his future interests are concerned.

Similarly, those Snakes seeking work or wanting to change their present position should remain alert for opportunities to pursue. Positive action on their part will bring results and it would be in their interests to be adven-turous in the types of position they seek. The Snake has many talents and in the Rat year he should make sure he uses and promotes them as much as he can.

The Snake will fare reasonably well in financial matters at this time and many Snakes can look forward to an upturn in their financial situation. However, the Snake should not let any improvement persuade him into buying unnecessary items or being too indulgent. If he is able to set some money aside for a specific purpose or make some savings, he should do so.

The Snake's domestic life will be particularly active towards the end of the year and while there will be many demands on his time, both his family and close friends will give him much pleasure. A family party or gathering held late in the year is also likely to prove most memorable, especially as many Snakes will have the opportunity to meet up with some friends or relations they have not seen for some time.

Generally the Rat year will have been a positive year for the Snake but it will also have been a demanding one and it is important that he does not neglect his well-being. Despite the many demands on his time, he should make sure he continues with his hobbies and recreational interests and gives himself the chance to relax and unwind regularly. The Snake does not have the stamina of some and to drive himself too hard could leave him feeling tired and not making as much of himself as he otherwise could. As the Rat year draws to a close, the Snake should make sure he gives himself a decent break, particularly over the Christmas and New Year holidays. After all he has accomplished in the Rat year, he deserves one!

The Year of the Ox starts on 7 February and will be a fair year for the Snake. He can enjoy a reasonable amount of success but to achieve results he will need to work hard and concentrate on specific matters. To take things leisurely – as some Snakes could be tempted to do – or spread his energies too widely will lead to disappointing results. This can be a positive year but it is one in which the Snake does need to apply himself.

Indeed, after the activity of the Rat year, the Snake would do well to reflect upon his present position and decide what it is he next wishes to attain. He should consolidate any recent gains and give thought to his future priorities. In this he would also do well to discuss his ideas with those around him and listen closely to the advice he is given, particularly from those who speak with experience. Sometimes the Snake has a tendency to keep himself to himself and a too solitary or independent an attitude could undermine his progress during the year. In 1997 he needs to work in conjunction with others rather than rely so heavily upon his own judgement.

When making plans for the year the Snake should be realistic in his undertakings. In his work he should stick to areas in which he is most familiar rather than be over-ambitious and try for something for which he does not have the necessary experience. He should also be wary of committing himself to anything too risky. The Snake can make progress over the year but it will come from sensible planning and hard work rather than from chance.

Also, in his work the Snake needs to pay close attention to all that is going on around him and be prepared to adapt to changing situations. Although he may hold firm views on what he wants to accomplish, to remain intransigent or stubborn could be to his detriment as well as affect the normally good relations he enjoys with his colleagues. In 1997 the Snake will need to tread warily and remain his usual diplomatic self!

However, while there is a certain need for caution over the year, this should not prevent the Snake from furthering his ideas. Provided he is prepared to work hard and set about his activities in a positive manner he can make reasonable progress. The Ox year, with its emphasis on duty, does favour those who are prepared to work and this can, if he is prepared to make the effort, include the Snake! Indeed, some of the ideas that he develops over the year will find favour with others and he should be forthcoming with any ideas that occur to him. Similarly, if he wants to further his experience or is seeking work, the Snake should pursue any opportunities that interest him. Admittedly, not all his endeavours may meet with success and there will be times when he will feel despondent about his lack of progress, but providing he perseveres he will eventually get what he wants. The Snake's employment prospects will improve as the year goes on and the period from September to December will mark an upturn in work matters.

The Snake should also take advantage of any opportunity to go on courses that he might be eligible for. Or, if there is a subject that has been interesting him, this would be an ideal year to find out more. As far as the Snake is concerned, 1997 is an excellent year for adding to his skills and qualifications and he will find that this will do much to enhance his prospects. In addition, the challenge of learning a new subject or skill will be both stimulating and satisfying for him.

The Snake is usually astute when dealing with financial matters but throughout the Ox year he does need to be on his guard. This is not a time when he can afford to take unnecessary risks or become too complacent in his financial dealings. If he enters into any large transaction, he should check the terms of the agreement carefully and be aware of any obligations he may be placed under. He should also be wary of any highly speculative venture that he hears about, no matter how tempting it might at first appear. If he is not his usual careful self, he could incur some financial misfortune over the year and to avoid this it is essential he remains vigilant.

In addition to this need for caution in work and financial matters, the Snake will also need to exercise care in his relations with others. This includes family, friends and colleagues. Over the year the Snake must be more prepared to involve those around him in his activities. Sometimes his preference for doing things his own way or all by himself can work against him and this could well be the case in the Ox year. Throughout he needs to remain mindful of the views and feelings of those around him. If he bears this in mind, he will do much to minimize some of the more negative aspects that prevail.

However, in spite of this, the Snake can still look forward to some enjoyable family occasions and there will also be good cause for both personal and family rejoicing over the summer months. The Snake would also do well to encourage joint activities with his family members, particularly with projects around the home and garden. He will find these will give all involved much satisfaction.

The Snake's social life will also provide him with much pleasure and for unattached or lonely Snakes there will be some excellent opportunities to make new friends as the year progresses. The months from May to August will, in particular, be a busy and enjoyable time for social matters.

Although travel may not figure too prominently over

the year, the journeys and holidays that the Snake does take will generally go well. Many Snakes will particularly delight in a holiday they take in the second half of the year, especially if it is to a destination they have never visited before.

The Snake would also do well to consider taking up a new interest over the year and one that would give him a break from his usual everyday concerns. With his imaginative nature he could find a creative activity most satisfying for him. Also, if he does not get much exercise during the day, he should consider engaging in more outdoor and physical activities; anything positive that he can do to help his well-being will leave him feeling fitter and better able to give of his best.

While the Ox year may, in parts, be a variable year for the Snake, it need not be a bad one. Provided he plans his activities well, works hard and remains his usual careful self, he can make progress. However, if he takes risks or chooses to ignore the advice and views of others, then he could find himself running into problems. Just how much the Snake achieves and succeeds over the year is very much in his own hands.

As far as the different types of Snake are concerned, this will be an important year for the *Metal Snake*. He will have cause to reflect on his present position and to think over what he wishes to do both in this and future years. In making his plans he should discuss his ideas with those closest to him and while he does have a tendency to keep his thoughts to himself, in 1997 he will be very much helped by the input of others. In making any plans, however, he should not take any irrevocable action until he is satisfied in his own mind that it is the right course to take and neither should he take snap decisions. Time is on his side and the plans he makes – whether they involve a change in his occupation, his accommodation or some other matter – will generally work in his favour. While 1997 may not be the smoothest of years for the Metal Snake, the long-term effects of the year will prove positive and significant. In his work the Metal Snake may have difficulty in achieving all that he would like. Some of his plans may be affected by delays, the opposition of others or changed circumstances. However, while this may prove frustrating at the time, provided the Metal Snake is prepared to adapt to changing situations and continues to set about his activities in his usual thorough manner, he can still make creditable progress. He should, however, remain mindful of the views and opinions of his colleagues, and while he does possess a strong independent streak, he will find the best results will come from joining forces with others rather than relying solely upon his own individual efforts. The Metal Snake would also do well to look closely at his financial situation over the year and examine his regular outgoings. He could find some of these are no longer necessary and that a few modifications could make a noticeable difference. Also, if he is able to set some spare money aside for his longer term future he could be grateful for this in years to come. The Metal Snake's domestic life will give him much satisfaction over the year and he will take considerable pleasure in the achievements of those close to him. He will also find that family outings and any holidays he takes will go well. However, during the first part of the year, he may have to help a relative or close friend who has an awkward problem to overcome. Any assistance he is able to give will be truly valued, probably more than he may realize at the time. Many do value the Metal Snake's clear-sightedness and judgement and this will be particularly the case in 1997. The Metal Snake will also derive much pleasure from his various interests and hobbies over the year, especially any of a creative nature or that take him out-of-doors. Any Metal Snake who is a keen collector, particularly of antiques or *objets d'art*, or who wants to buy some new home furnishings could be fortunate in some purchases at this time. The Metal Snake possesses good taste and a shrewd eye and these will certainly not let him down over the year. Generally, while not all the events of the year may proceed as smoothly or as rapidly as he would like, 1997 will still contain many pleasurable times for the Metal Snake. But throughout the year he does need to remain mindful of others and be prepared to adapt to changing situations.

This can be a constructive year for the *Water Snake*, although how much he does achieve is heavily dependent upon his own efforts. In the Ox year the Water Snake will find that hard work will bring positive results – but it must be emphasized that it will require much effort on his part to obtain the results he desires. If he is prepared to work hard and make the most of his considerable abilities, he can do extremely well. In particular, he will be able to consolidate and build on gains he has made in recent years and will be offered several excellent opportunities as a result of his labours. For the bold, enterprising and assertive Water Snake, this can be a year of considerable potential and he can go a long way towards achieving his ambitions and improving his current position. However, if the Water Snake decides to rest content with his present situation – as he may be tempted to do – then his progress will not nearly be so great and he could miss out on some otherwise good opportunities. The manner in which the year proceeds, particularly as far as his work interests are concerned, is very much dependent upon the Water Snake himself. The opportunities are certainly there if he is prepared to work for them. Those Water Snakes who are dissatisfied with their present position or are seeking employment should actively follow up any openings that they see. Again, determined effort will bring results and the later months of the Ox year will prove a most positive time for work matters. The Water Snake's domestic life will be busy over the year but those around him will bring him much pleasure. He will delight in the progress and accomplishments of those close to him and when he does find himself with a lot to do, especially in the way of household chores, he should not hesitate to ask for assistance. He will find this readily forthcoming. The Water Snake should also try to be more open with his ideas and thoughts than he tends to be; his family and friends do want to encourage and support him, but for them to be able to do this, they do need to be more aware of what is going through his complex and often secretive mind. The Water Snake should also make sure that he sets a regular time aside for his hobbies and interests over the year, particularly those that enable him to relax and unwind. This will generally be a demanding year for him and he does need to take good care of himself. To drive himself too hard could leave him tired and lacking in energy as well as susceptible to minor ailments. In the Ox year he cannot afford to ignore or neglect his well-being. Generally, however, if the Water Snake takes the year sensibly and sets about his activities and work diligently then this can be a productive and successful year for him.

This will be a varied but interesting year for the *Wood Snake*. Several opportunities will present themselves which will cause him to review his plans and longer term aims. Admittedly some of the opportunities that occur, particularly involving his work, may not be quite in the capacity that he may have originally envisaged, but he should regard them as chances for him to usefully extend his experience. However, in all that he does in the Ox year, the Wood Snake will be helped by his versatility, good judgement and ability to get on with others. The second half of the year will be a particularly good time for him to further his career interests and it is then that the Wood Snake should remain alert for chances to improve upon his present position and to promote his ideas. Those Wood Snakes seeking employment should remain active in following up any openings that they see and many will find their quest for work rewarded in quite an unexpected way! As all Snakes will find in 1997, determined effort will result in positive progress. In addition to what the Wood Snake achieves in his work, he would also do well to consider extending his skills and qualifications. Learning a new subject could usefully occupy some of his spare time and provide him with an interesting challenge as well as do much to enhance and assist his prospects. The Wood Snake will fare well in financial matters over the year, although it would be in his interests to keep a close watch over his level of expenditure. In particular, he should resist being overly indulgent or extravagant in his spending. Without care he could find himself having to dip into his savings when they could be put to better use, such as household improvements or travel. The Wood Snake's domestic life will be busy and often demanding, with many household matters especially requiring his attention, but he can still look forward to many pleasurable occasions. His family will also be most supportive and in view of some of the decisions that he has to take, particularly involving work matters, he would do well to discuss his options with them and listen closely to their views. They do speak with his best interests at heart and some advice that he is given by someone older than himself will prove particularly pertinent. He will also enjoy outdoor pursuits over the year and for Wood Snakes who are keen gardeners or have sporting interests, the year will contain some rewarding moments. Generally, this can be a satisfying year for the Wood Snake and providing he is prepared to embrace the opportunities he sees, he can turn it into a significant one which will have positive and far-reaching consequences.

The *Fire Snake* has many fine qualities. He is quick thinking, ambitious and determined to make the most of himself and his abilities. However, despite his noble intentions, he will have to proceed steadily over the year. Although he may have many grand ideas about what he wants to accomplish, some of these require experience he has not yet obtained and he could find he is trying to undertake too much too soon. In 1997 the Fire Snake needs to be realistic in his objectives and aim to build on his experience rather than launch forth on ambitious under-takings. This will be more a year for learning and for steady rather than for rapid progress. All Fire Snakes, whether in work or seeking work, should do all they can over the year to extend their skills and if they are eligible for any courses, they should follow them up. The experi-ence that the Fire Snake gains in 1997 will hold him in good stead for the future. In his work he should set about his duties in his usual conscientious way and show himself adaptable to the various tasks he is asked to carry out. This way he will impress those with influence and again this will be to his longer-term advantage. The first few months of the year and the period from September to November will prove significant times for career matters. As far as his finances are concerned, the Fire Snake should keep a watchful eye on his level of spending. Many Fire Snakes could be involved in a large transaction over the year, particularly connected with their accommodation, and they do need to make sure they can meet the obligations that they may be placed under. Fortunately the Fire Snake is usually astute when dealing with matters of finance, but care is needed. Personally, however, the Ox year will contain some happy and special times. The Fire Snake's social life will be active and there will be many opportuni-ties for romance and for making new friends. A large number of Fire Snakes will marry in the Ox year. Any Fire Snake who has moved to a new area, is feeling lonely or has had some recent sadness to bear should make every effort to join a local society or group where he can meet others. Socially, this can be a good year for him and it would be in his interests to get in contact with others. The

Fire Snake will enjoy any travelling that he undertakes in 1997 and his interests, too, will provide him with many hours of pleasure. Again, if he can meet up with others who share his interests, he could find this will not only increase and broaden his knowledge but result in some meaningful and in some cases long-lasting friendships. Generally, 1997 will be a pleasant year for the Fire Snake, but as far as work matters are concerned, he does need to be realistic in his expectations. This is a year for gaining knowledge and experience and once he has this behind him, then he will begin to make the progress he so much desires. In the meantime, patience, dear Fire Snake, patience!

This will be a variable year for the *Earth Snake* and while it will certainly contain some pleasurable moments, he could find it difficult to achieve all he would like. Some of his plans may take him longer to carry out than he anticipated and in some cases he may have to revise his ideas. In 1997 the Earth Snake needs to keep his expectations modest and exercise patience with some of his undertakings. He will, however, be greatly helped by the support and co-operation that he receives from his family and close friends and should he find himself in a dilemma over any matter he should not hesitate to seek advice. Although some Earth Snakes may feel that others do not want to be bothered with their concerns, this is just not the case. Their family and friends are keen to help them and throughout the year Earth Snakes will be grateful for the assistance they receive. Any problems that do arise are more likely to be nigglesome than serious and in some cases the Earth Snake could even find that he is worrying unnecessarily.

He is, however, one who always uses his time wisely and he will be pleased with some of the projects that he carries out on his home and garden. He will also take considerable delight in the activities and achievements of those around him, and domestically and socially the year will generally go well. In addition, he should take advantage of any opportunity to meet up with friends or relations he has not seen for some time. Such a meeting will give all concerned much pleasure. Although the Earth Snake may not travel too far over the year, he could find short outings, particularly to places of local interest, especially enjoyable. While Ox year may not be entirely trouble-free for the Earth Snake, it will still be one he will generally enjoy.

FAMOUS SNAKES

Muhammad Ali, Ann-Margret, Yasser Arafat, Paddy Ashdown, Ronnie Barker, Kim Basinger, Benazir Bhutto, Bjork, Tony Blair, William Blake, Heinrich Böll, Betty Boothroyd, Brahms, Pierce Brosnan, Will Carling, Chubby Checker, Tom Conti, Randy Crawford, Jim Davidson, Bob Dylan, Elgar, Sir Alexander Fleming, Henry Fonda, Mahatma Gandhi, Greta Garbo, Art Garfunkel, J. Paul Getty, Dizzy Gillespie, W. E. Gladstone, Goethe, Princess Grace of Monaco, Stephen Hawking, Nigel Hawthorne, Lord Healey, Audrey Hepburn, Jack Higgins, Paul Hogan, Michael Howard, Howard Hughes, Rev. Jesse Jackson, Stacy Keach, Howard Keel, J. F. Kennedy, Carole King, James Last, Cindi Lauper, Dame Vera Lynn, Linda McCartney, Craig McLachlan, Magnus Magnusson, Mao Tse-tung, Nigel Mansell, Henri Matisse, Sir Patrick Mayhew, Sarah Miles, Robert Mitchum, Nasser, Bob Newhart, Mike Oldfield, Aristotle Onassis, Jacqueline Onassis, Ryan O'Neal, Dorothy Parker, Pablo Picasso, Mary Pickford, Michael Portillo, André Previn, Helen Reddy, Griff Rhys Jones, Franklin D. Roosevelt, Mickey Rourke, Jean-Paul Sartre, Franz Schubert, Brooke Shields, Nigel Short, Paul Simon, Delia Smith, John Thaw, Dionne Warwick, Charlie Watts, Ruby Wax, Oprah Winfrey, Victoria Wood, Virginia Woolf, Susannah York.

25 JANUARY 1906 〜 12 FEBRUARY 1907   *Fire Horse*

11 FEBRUARY 1918 〜 31 JANUARY 1919   *Earth Horse*

30 JANUARY 1930 〜 16 FEBRUARY 1931   *Metal Horse*

15 FEBRUARY 1942 〜 4 FEBRUARY 1943   *Water Horse*

3 FEBRUARY 1954 〜 23 JANUARY 1955   *Wood Horse*

21 JANUARY 1966 〜 8 FEBRUARY 1967   *Fire Horse*

7 FEBRUARY 1978 〜 27 JANUARY 1979   *Earth Horse*

27 JANUARY 1990 〜 14 FEBRUARY 1991   *Metal Horse*

THE
HORSE

THE PERSONALITY OF THE HORSE

Experience is not what happens to a man. It is what a man does with what happens to him.

– Aldous Huxley: a Horse

The Horse is born under the signs of elegance and ardour. He has a most engaging and charming manner and is usually very popular. He loves meeting people and likes attending parties and other large social gatherings.

He is a lively character and enjoys being the centre of attention. He has considerable leadership qualities and is much admired for his honest and straightforward manner. He is an eloquent and persuasive speaker and has a great love of discussion and debate. The Horse also has a particularly agile mind and can assimilate facts remarkably quickly.

He does, however, have a fiery temper and although his outbursts are usually short-lived, he can often say things which he will later regret. He is also not particularly good at keeping secrets.

The Horse has many interests and involves himself in a wide variety of activities. He can, however, get involved in so much that he can often waste his energies on projects which he never has time to complete. He also has a tendency to change his interests rather frequently and will often get caught up with the latest craze or 'in thing' until something better or more exciting turns up.

The Horse also likes to have a certain amount of freedom and independence in the things that he does. He hates being bound by petty rules and regulations and as far as possible likes to feel that he is answerable to no one but himself. But despite this spirit of freedom, he still likes to have the support and encouragement of others in his various enterprises.

Due to his many talents and likeable nature, the Horse will often go far in life. He enjoys challenges and is a methodical and tireless worker. However, should things work against him and he fail in any of his enterprises, it will take a long time for him to recover and pick up the pieces again. Success to the Horse means everything. To fail is a disaster and a humiliation.

The Horse likes to have variety in his life and he will try his hand at many different things before he settles down to one particular job. Even then, he will probably remain alert to see whether there are any new and better opportunities for him to take up. The Horse has a restless nature and can easily get bored. He does, however, excel in any position which allows him sufficient freedom to act on his own initiative or which brings him into contact with a lot of people.

Although the Horse is not particularly bothered about accumulating great wealth, he handles his finances with care and will rarely experience any serious financial problems.

The Horse also enjoys travel and he loves visiting new and far-away places. At some stage during his life he will be tempted to live abroad for a short period of time and due to his adaptable nature he will find that he will fit in well wherever he goes.

The Horse pays a great deal of attention to his appearance and usually likes to wear smart, colourful and rather distinctive clothes. He is very attractive to the opposite sex and will often have many romances before he settles down. He is loyal and protective to his partner, but, despite his family commitments, still likes to retain a certain measure of independence and have the freedom to carry on with his own interests and hobbies. He will find that he is especially well-suited to those born under the signs of the Tiger, Goat, Rooster and Dog. The Horse can also get on well with the Rabbit, Dragon, Snake, Pig and another Horse, but he will find the Ox too serious and intolerant for his liking. The Horse will also have difficulty in getting on with the Monkey and the Rat – the Monkey is very inquisitive and the Rat seeks security, and both will resent the Horse's rather independent ways.

The female Horse is usually most attractive and has a friendly, outgoing personality. She is highly intelligent, has many interests and is alert to everything that is going on around her. She particularly enjoys outdoor pursuits and often likes to take part in sport and keep-fit activities. She also enjoys travel, literature and the arts, and is a very good conversationalist.

Although the Horse can be stubborn and rather self-centred, he does have a considerate nature and is often willing to help others. He has a good sense of humour and will usually make a favourable impression wherever he goes. Provided he can curb his slightly restless nature and keep a tight control over his temper, he will go through life making friends, taking part in a multitude of different activities and generally achieving many of his objectives. His life will rarely be dull.

THE FIVE DIFFERENT TYPES
OF HORSE

In addition to the 12 signs of the Chinese zodiac, there are five elements, and these have a strengthening or moderating influence on the sign. The effects of the five elements on the Horse are described below, together with the years in which the elements were exercising their influence. Therefore all Horses born in 1930 and 1990 are Metal Horses, those born in 1942 are Water Horses and so on.

Metal Horse: 1930, 1990

This Horse is bold, confident and forthright. He is ambitious and also a great innovator. He loves challenges and takes great delight in sorting out complicated problems. He likes to have a certain amount of independence in the things that he does and resents any outside interference. The Metal Horse has charm and a certain charisma, but he can also be very stubborn and rather impulsive. He usually has many friends and enjoys an active social life.

Water Horse: 1942

The Water Horse has a friendly nature, a good sense of humour, and is able to talk intelligently on a wide range of topics. He is astute in business matters and quick to take advantage of any opportunities that arise. He does, however, have a tendency to get easily distracted and can change his interests – and indeed his mind – rather frequently, and this can sometimes work to his detriment. He is nevertheless very talented and can often go far in life. He pays a great deal of attention to his appearance and is usually smart and well turned out. He loves to travel and also enjoys sport and other outdoor activities.

Wood Horse: 1894, 1954

The Wood Horse has a most agreeable and amiable nature. He communicates well with others and, like the Water Horse, is able to talk intelligently on many different subjects. He is a hard and conscientious worker and is held in high esteem by his friends and colleagues. His opinions and views are often sought and, given his imaginative nature, he can quite often come up with some very original and practical ideas. He is usually widely read and likes to lead a busy social life. He can also be most generous and often holds high moral viewpoints.

Fire Horse: 1906, 1966

The element of Fire combined with the temperament of the Horse creates one of the most powerful forces in the Chinese zodiac. The Fire Horse is destined to lead an exciting and eventful life and to make his mark in his chosen profession. He has a forceful personality and his intelligence and resolute manner bring him the support and admiration of many. He loves action and excitement and his life will rarely be quiet. He can, however, be rather blunt and forthright in his views and does not take kindly to interference in his own affairs or to obeying orders. He is a flamboyant character, has a good sense of humour and will lead a very active social life.

Earth Horse: 1918, 1978

This Horse is considerate and caring. He is more cautious than some of the other types of Horse, but he is wise, perceptive and extremely capable. Although he can be rather indecisive at times, he has considerable business acumen and is very astute in financial matters. He has a quiet, friendly nature and is well thought of by his family and friends.

PROSPECTS FOR THE HORSE IN 1997

The Chinese New Year starts on 7 February 1997. Until then, the old year, the Year of the Rat, is still making its presence felt.

The Year of the Rat (19 February 1996 to 6 February 1997) will not have been the easiest of years for the Horse and in what remains of it he will still need to exercise care in most of his activities. This is just not a year when he can take risks or be too independent in his actions. Also, to preserve the normally good relations he enjoys with those around him, he must remain mindful of the views of family, friends and colleagues and keep his volatile Horse temper in check!

However, while the Horse may not always be able to make as much progress as he would like in the Rat year, it can still be a constructive one for him. He should embrace any opportunity to add to his experience and it is also an ideal time to take up a new interest, whether vocational or purely as a hobby. What the Horse learns and commences now could prove of considerable value to him in years to come.

The Horse should also reflect upon his present situation and give some thought to his future. Some of the ideas and plans he formulates in the latter part of the Rat year will turn out to be most significant in the next Chinese year. In particular, the months from September to November 1996 will be a constructive time for him, especially for work and work-related activities. It is also at this time that he should promote any ideas he has or pursue any openings that would help improve his present position.

The Horse does, however, need to exercise care when dealing with financial matters. He should be wary of getting involved in risky undertakings and would do well to keep a watchful eye on his level of spending. The last two months of the Rat year can be an expensive time for him and to avoid running into difficulties later, he needs to make allowances for any extra outlay he makes. Provided he is careful, all will be well, but, as with most things in the Rat year, the Horse needs to be vigilant.

Domestically and socially, the Horse can look forward to some enjoyable times with those around him in the last few months of the Rat year. His family and social life will be busy and pleasurable and a relation or close friend could have some encouraging news for him in December. For the young and unattached Horse this will also prove a favourable time.

Although the Horse may not have achieved all that he would have liked in the Year of the Rat, the experience he has gained and any ideas he has formulated will hold him in good stead for the future, especially for the more productive Ox year.

The Year of the Ox starts on 7 February and will be a considerably improved year for the Horse. After the problems and uncertainties of the Rat year, he can look forward to an upturn in his fortunes and, as far as his work and finances are concerned, this will be a rewarding year for him.

In 1997 the Horse will be able to put his experience and skills to good use and many Horses will make progress in their work. The Ox year favours those who are industrious and work well and this certainly applies to the Horse. Horses who are wanting to gain a better position or seeking work should go after any available openings and also see if they can create some opportunities themselves. If they can think of a way they can put their skills and experience to good use, they should contact those who may be interested or who may be able to help them. Some lateral and innovative thinking on the Horse's part could lead to some splendid results! This is very much a year when enterprise and hard work will pay off and by acting determinedly almost all Horses will be able to improve upon their current situation during the year.

In addition to the positive progress that the Horse can make in his work, those Horses in education will also do well and by setting about their studies in a determined and persistent manner can achieve good results.

However, while the aspects are favourable for the Horse in the Ox year, there is one point that he should bear in mind. As a Horse he is likely to have wide and varied interests and there could be a temptation for him to involve himself in too many activities at the same time. If possible he should resist this. To spread his energies too widely could limit his progress and he will find he will fare better if he concentrates his efforts on specific activities. He could find it helpful to remember the proverb 'Better be master than jack of all trades.'

The Horse will also enjoy good fortune in financial matters and any Horse who may have been experiencing financial problems will find these will ease as the year progresses. Some Horses will enjoy a noticeable increase in their salary over the year while others may receive some money from an unexpected source. If the Horse is able to put any spare money he has towards a specific purpose or start a regular savings scheme he will be well pleased with just how much he is able to accumulate. Some investments that he makes in 1997 could also prove successful and he could make some pleasing purchases both for himself and for his home. He should particularly keep alert for items during shop sales as he is likely to spot some excellent bargains at these times. Generally, matters to do with finance will go well for him.

However, while his work and finances are favourably aspected, the Horse does need to handle his relations with others with care. In all his undertakings he needs to work closely with those around him and be forthcoming about his views and plans. Sometimes this means he will have to forsake the independence he values so much, but this is just not a year when he can risk jeopardizing the normally good relations he enjoys with so many. It is very much a year for co-operation and teamwork. The Horse will, in any case, benefit from the input of others and throughout the year he should pay close attention to any advice he is given, particularly from those older than himself who speak with the benefit of experience.

The Horse should also avoid the temptation of becoming so preoccupied with his own concerns that he does not devote as much attention to his family and friends as he should. If he is not careful, tensions could result. Throughout the year he would do well to take a close interest in the activities of those around him. It would also be helpful if he were to encourage some joint projects around the house or garden, particularly those that would give both himself and his family satisfaction in carrying out. Family holidays or outings will prove pleasurable, but again the Horse would do well to encourage activities that those around him would enjoy. His family means much to him but in the Ox year he must make sure he does not neglect their interests. To do so could sour an otherwise good year for him.

The Horse should also not take his friends for granted. They think highly of him, but he does need to remain mindful of their views and give them both his time and attention. They are prepared to help and support him, but they do expect something in return! Similarly, for the unattached Horse, care is needed in his relations with others and Horses seeking new friendships and romance should let any new friendship develop gradually rather than rush into a commitment after just a short meeting. As far as romance and matters of the heart are concerned, the Horse must tread carefully and sensibly.

Also, should the Horse find himself in any contentious situation over the year, he would do well to exercise tact and discretion. In the case of a disagreement arising, he should seek a compromise or solution agreeable to all rather than remain intransigent or unduly stubborn. Generally, the Horse can have some enjoyable times in the Ox year but he does need to be careful in matters concerning his relations with others.

As this will be quite an active year for the Horse, he should also make sure that he devotes time to his own interests, particularly those that enable him to have a break from his everyday duties. He will find out-of-door activities particularly pleasurable and for Horses who do not get much exercise during the day, some additional walking or activities such as cycling or swimming will prove beneficial. Travel is also well aspected and, if possible, the Horse should try to make sure he goes away for at least one break over the year.

Generally, 1997 can be a positive year for the Horse. He can look forward to making significant progress in his work and to an improvement in his financial situation. In his work, he should promote himself and his skills as much as he can and will find positive action on his part will bring pleasing results. However, in his relations with others he must exercise care. In 1997 he should remain mindful of the views of all around him and be prepared to act in conjunction with others rather than independently. This is a year for tact and discretion. If the Horse bears this in mind, it can be both a productive and rewarding one for him.

As far as the different types of Horse are concerned, this will be an active and generally pleasant year for the *Metal Horse*. In 1997 he will obtain particular satisfaction from his interests, some of which could even prove remunerative for him. Over the year he would do well to contact others who share his interests as this will lead to a furthering of his own knowledge and to some highly pleasurable social occasions. Those Metal Horses who enjoy writing or whose hobbies involve the creative arts should also promote their work as it is likely to be well received. In addition to the satisfaction that the Metal Horse will obtain from his interests, the year favours travel and he will greatly enjoy any journeys, holidays and breaks he takes. If there is some destination that he has longed to visit or there are some friends he would like to see that he has not seen for some time, this would be an ideal year to do so. The Metal Horse will also enjoy an improvement in his financial situation over the year and if he finds he has some additional funds at his disposal, he should make sure he puts these to good use. In particular he will be pleased with some items he acquires which will do much to improve both the décor and comfort of his home. He will also spend some of his spare time in decorating and DIY projects. While he will be satisfied with the result, he should be careful when using dangerous pieces of equipment and moving heavy items. A strain could cause him some discomfort and when engaging in any hazardous activity the Metal Horse must make sure he follows all the precautions necessary. As far as his relations with others are concerned, he needs to remain mindful of the opinions and views of those around him. While he himself may hold very firm ideas, he cannot expect to have things all his own way! In case of disagreement, he would do well to seek a solution acceptable to all, even if it means giving way on a certain point, rather than remain intransigent. To do otherwise could result in domestic tensions and take the edge off the year. It is in this area of personal relations that the Metal Horse needs to exercise greatest care. Providing he does, this will be a year which he will find both enjoyable and satisfying.

This will be a positive and practical year for the *Water Horse* and he is likely to make good progress in many of his activities. In his work, in particular, there will be changes in store and many Water Horses will take on new and increased responsibilities as the year progresses. Some events will come as surprises, but provided the Water Horse is prepared to be adaptable in his outlook, he will rise up to the challenges given him and do well. Throughout the year he will also be helped by his versatility and some skills he has not used for some time could turn out to be highly useful to him. For Water Horses seeking work or wanting to change their present position, the year will offer several openings to pursue; again, if they can draw on past experience and show themselves adaptable in the type of position they seek, their quest for work or a change could prove successful. The Water Horse will also enjoy good fortune in financial matters and most Water Horses will end the year in a much improved financial position. They would do well to consider putting any spare money they do have towards a specific purpose rather than spending it needlessly, particularly as they could make some splendid purchases that could add to the comfort of their home. Domestically, though, this will be a demanding year and there are likely to be several important family matters that will require the Water Horse's attention. Should any matters cause him concern, he should let his feelings be known rather than keep them to himself. Also, he should try to resolve any disagreement as quickly and amicably as he can rather than allow it to linger in the background. He should also make every effort to involve those around him in his own activities as well as take an active interest in what others are doing. To become too preoccupied with his own concerns could lead to some tensions. Provided the Water Horse is his usual considerate self and is open and forthcoming with others, his domestic life can go well and bring him much satisfaction, but care is needed. The Water Horse will also get much pleasure from the time he spends on his various interests over the year as well as enjoy and obtain much benefit from the travelling that he undertakes. Generally, 1997 will be a productive year for him and will contain several opportunities for him to improve upon his present position. But as with all Horses in the Ox year, the Water Horse will need to exercise care in the area of personal relations. If he heeds this advice, then 1997 can be a progressive and pleasing year for him.

This will be a constructive year for the *Wood Horse*. Over the course of it he will see several changes take place, especially involving his work. Some of these changes will be unexpected and may initially give him some misgivings, but throughout the Ox year the Wood Horse will find that out of change will come new opportunities. They will also help to give him a renewed incentive to make the most of himself and he will take much satisfaction in rising to the challenges and opportunities that the year brings. The months from February to June will be particularly active for career matters and those Wood Horses seeking work or a change in work could make good progress at this time. All Wood Horses would also do well to take advantage of any chance they get to extend their skills over the year or enrol on courses that they feel would be of future benefit to them. This will be an important year for the Wood Horse and he should make the most of the encouraging trends that prevail. Also his accomplishments in the Ox year will help to sow the seeds for the considerably greater advances he can look forward to in 1998. The Wood Horse will also enjoy an improvement in his financial situation and could do well with an investment that he makes or a savings policy that he starts over the year. In view of the active nature of the year, however, the Wood Horse may not always feel he has as much time for his hobbies and interests as he would like, but it is important that he does not neglect them. His hobbies do provide him with an important source of relaxation and he could find activities of a creative nature, such as painting, writing, photography or music, particularly satisfying. The Wood Horse can also look forward to some pleasing times with his family and friends but, as with all Horses, he does need to handle his relations with others with care and exercise tact should any fraught situation arise. To impair relations by a thoughtless remark or heated exchange could easily sour what will otherwise be a promising and fulfilling year for him.

This can be a highly successful year for the *Fire Horse*

and, with the right attitude, he can accomplish much. He is blessed with many fine abilities and has a sharp and alert mind. His problem, though, is his restlessness and tendency either to take on too much at any one time or to jump from one activity to another. Provided he limits his commitments over the year and concentrates on specific activities, however, he will enjoy considerable success. In his work his skills and diligence will be recognized and many Fire Horses will be given increased responsibilities while other Fire Horses will be successful in obtaining a new position. This will not only broaden their experience but lead to yet further opportunities for advancement towards the end of the year and in 1998. Almost all Fire Horses can achieve much in their work but to make the most of these favourable trends the Fire Horse needs to remain committed to his objectives, give of his best and not over-commit himself. He will also enjoy an upturn in his financial situation over the year. However, he should make sure he puts any spare money he has to a specific purpose rather than spend it needlessly. With travel well aspected, the Fire Horse could satisfy his curiosity by visiting a place he has wanted to see for some time or, alternatively, consider moving or improving his accommodation. By putting his finances to good use he will be pleased with the result, but he should be wary of letting any spare money he has slip through his hands on unnecessary purchases or needless extravagances. The Fire Horse can also look forward to an active domestic and social life and the year will contain some memorable moments for him. A younger relation in particular will be a great source of pride to him and any additional assistance he feels able to give to family members will be truly valued. However, although the Fire Horse has very set ideas on household matters, he cannot expect to prevail all the time. To avoid tense situations arising, he should listen to others and be prepared to show some flexibility when making plans involving those around him. If he bears this in mind, then this will be a satisfying and pleasant year for him.

This will be an important year for the *Earth Horse*. During the year he can make considerable progress, win new friends and impress those with influence. However, to make the most of the favourable trends that prevail, he needs to decide how best he wishes to use his talents. Early in the year he would do well to draw up some objectives and once he has decided what he wishes to do, he should pursue his objectives in a purposeful and determined manner. Without any such plan, he could so easily drift and not make the most of himself or the encouraging trends that prevail. There will certainly be several openings for him to pursue in his work and he would do well to remain alert for chances which would allow him to extend his experience and improve his position. Many Earth Horses will also find that one opportunity will lead to another and by giving of their best and being adaptable in their manner, they can do well. The months of March and April and the period from September to November could prove significant for career matters. Those Earth Horses in education are also likely to make excellent progress and while there will be times of pressure, the time and effort they put into their studies will repay them handsomely in future years. The Earth Horse will fare reasonably well in financial matters, although he should be wary about stretching his resources too far. If he enters into any large financial transaction over the year, especially connected with his accommodation, he should make sure he is aware of any obligations he may be placed under. He will thoroughly enjoy the travelling that he undertakes in 1997 and for those Earth Horses wanting to go abroad to improve their language skills or embark on lengthy travels, this could be a good year to do so. As with most of his activities in the Ox year, the Earth Horse will find positive action will bring favourable results. His personal life will also prove memorable and many Earth Horses will meet their future partner, get engaged or married over the year. However, while there will be times of personal joy in 1997, the Earth Horse should take careful note of some important advice he is given by an older relative. Although he may not agree with all he is told, there will be much wisdom in their words and they do speak with his best interests at heart. To ignore the views and advice of those senior to him, as well as close to him, could result in acrimony and this is something the Earth Horse would do well to avoid. Generally, however, the year holds much potential for him and by giving of his best and remaining alert to all around him he can and will do well.

FAMOUS HORSES

Neil Armstrong, Rowan Atkinson, Cheryl Baker, Margaret Beckett, Samuel Beckett, Ingmar Bergman, Leonard Bernstein, Sir John Betjeman, Karen Black, Helena Bonham-Carter, Leonid Brezhnev, Eric Cantona, Ray Charles, Chopin, Sean Connery, Billy Connolly, Catherine Cookson, Ronnie Corbett, Elvis Costello, Kevin Costner, Michael Crichton, James Dean, Les Dennis, Anne Diamond, Kirk Douglas, Robert Duvall, Clint Eastwood, Thomas Alva Edison, Britt Ekland, Chris Evans, Linda Evans, Chris Evert, Les Ferdinand, Ella Fitzgerald, Harrison Ford, Aretha Franklin, Sir Bob Geldof, Billy Graham, Sally Gunnell, Gene Hackman, Susan Hampshire, Rolf Harris, Rita Hayworth, Jimi Hendrix, Bob Hoskins, Ted Hughes, David Hunt, Douglas Hurd, Aldous Huxley, Janet Jackson, Nikita Khrushchev, Robert Kilroy-Silk, Neil Kinnock, Dr Helmut Kohl, Lenin, Annie Lennox, Desmond Lynam, Paul McCartney, Nelson Mandela, Princess Margaret, Curtis Mayfield, Spike Milligan, Ben Murphy, Jimmy Nail, Sir Isaac Newton, Sinead O'Connor, Louis Pasteur, Ross Perot, Harold Pinter, David Platt, Stephanie Powers, J. B. Priestley, Puccini, Claire Rayner, Rembrandt, Ruth Rendell, Jean Renoir, Theodore Roosevelt, Helena Rubenstein, Anwar Sadat, Sinatta, Peter Sissons, Lord Snowdon, Alexander Solzhenitsyn, Mickey Spillane, Lisa Stansfield, Earl Stockton, Barbra Streisand, Kiefer Sutherland, Patrick Swayze, John Travolta, Kathleen Turner, Mike Tyson, Vivaldi, Robert Wagner, Billy Wilder, Andy Williams, the Duke of Windsor, Steve Wright, Tammy Wynette, Boris Yeltsin, Michael York.

13 FEBRUARY 1907 ～ 1 FEBRUARY 1908	*Fire Goat*
1 FEBRUARY 1919 ～ 19 FEBRUARY 1920	*Earth Goat*
17 FEBRUARY 1931 ～ 5 FEBRUARY 1932	*Metal Goat*
5 FEBRUARY 1943 ～ 24 JANUARY 1944	*Water Goat*
24 JANUARY 1955 ～ 11 FEBRUARY 1956	*Wood Goat*
9 FEBRUARY 1967 ～ 29 JANUARY 1968	*Fire Goat*
28 JANUARY 1979 ～ 15 FEBRUARY 1980	*Earth Goat*
15 FEBRUARY 1991 ～ 3 FEBRUARY 1992	*Metal Goat*

THE
GOAT

THE PERSONALITY OF THE GOAT

Always do right. This will gratify some people and
astonish the rest.

— Mark Twain: a Goat

The Goat is born under the sign of art. He is imaginative,
creative and has a good appreciation of the finer things in
life. He has an easy-going nature and prefers to live in a
relaxed and pressure-free environment. He hates any sort
of discord or unpleasantness and does not like to be bound
by a strict routine or rigid timetable. The Goat is not one
to be hurried against his will but, despite his seemingly
relaxed approach to life, he is something of a perfectionist
and when he starts work on a project he is certain to give
of his best.

The Goat usually prefers to work in a team rather than
on his own. He likes to have the support and encouragement of others and if left to deal with matters on his own
he can get very worried and tends to view things rather
pessimistically. Wherever possible he will leave major
decision-making to others while he concentrates on his
own pursuits. If, however, he feels particularly strongly
about a certain matter or has to defend his position in any
way, he will act with great fortitude and precision.

The Goat has a very persuasive nature and often uses his
considerable charm to get his own way. He can, however,
be rather hesitant about letting his true feelings be known
and if he were prepared to be more forthright he would do
much better as a result.

The Goat tends to have a quiet, somewhat reserved nature but when he is in company he likes he can often become the centre of attention. He can be highly amusing, a marvellous host at parties and a superb entertainer. Whenever the spotlight falls on him, his adrenalin starts to flow and he can be assured of giving a sparkling performance, particularly if he is allowed to use his creative skills in any way.

Of all the signs in the Chinese zodiac, the Goat is probably the most gifted artistically. Whether it is in the theatre, literature, music or art, he is certain to make a lasting impression. He is a born creator and is rarely happier than when occupied in some artistic pursuit. But even in this, the Goat does well to work with others rather than on his own. He needs inspiration and a guiding influence, but when he has found his true *métier*, he can often receive widespread acclaim and recognition.

In addition to his liking for the arts, the Goat is usually quite religious and often has a deep interest in nature, animals and the countryside. He is also fairly athletic and there are many Goats who have excelled in some form of sporting activity.

Although the Goat is not particularly materialistic or concerned about finance, he will find that he will usually be lucky in financial matters and will rarely be short of the necessary funds to tide himself over. He is, however, rather indulgent and tends to spend his money as soon as he receives it rather than make provision for the future.

The Goat usually leaves home when he is young but he will always maintain strong links with his parents and the other members of his family. He is also rather nostalgic

YOUR CHINESE HOROSCOPE 1997

and is well known for keeping mementoes of his childhood and souvenirs of places that he has visited. His home will not be particularly tidy but he knows where everything is and it will also be scrupulously clean.

Affairs of the heart are particularly important to the Goat and he will often have many romances before he finally settles down. Although he is fairly adaptable, he prefers to live in a secure and stable environment and will find that he is best suited to those born under the signs of the Tiger, Horse, Monkey, Pig and Rabbit. He can also establish a good relationship with the Dragon, Snake, Rooster and another Goat, but he may find the Ox and Dog a little too serious for his liking. Neither will he care particularly for the Rat's rather thrifty ways.

The female Goat devotes all her time and energy to the needs of her family. She has excellent taste in home furnishings and often uses her considerable artistic skills to make clothes for herself and her children. She takes great care over her appearance and can be most attractive to the opposite sex. Although she is not the most well-organized of people, her engaging manner and delightful sense of humour create a favourable impression wherever she goes. She is also a good cook and usually gets much pleasure from gardening and outdoor pursuits.

The Goat can win friends easily and people generally feel relaxed in his company. He has a kind and under-standing nature and although he can occasionally be stub-born, he can, with the right support and encouragement, live a happy and very satisfying life. The more he can use his creative skills, the happier he will be.

THE FIVE DIFFERENT TYPES OF GOAT

In addition to the 12 signs of the Chinese zodiac, there are five elements, and these have a strengthening or moderating influence on the sign. The effects of the five elements on the Goat are described below, together with the years in which the elements were exercising their influence. Therefore all Goats born in 1931 and 1991 are Metal Goats, those born in 1943 are Water Goats, and so on.

Metal Goat: 1931, 1991

This Goat is thorough and conscientious in all that he does and is capable of doing very well in his chosen profession. Despite his confident manner, he can be a great worrier and he would find it a help to discuss his worries with others rather than keep them to himself. He is loyal to his family and employers and will have a small group of extremely good friends. He has good artistic taste and is usually highly skilled in some aspect of the arts. He is often a collector of antiques and his home will be very tastefully furnished.

Water Goat: 1943

The Water Goat is very popular and makes friends with remarkable ease. He is good at spotting opportunities but does not always have the necessary confidence to follow them through. He likes to have security both in his home life and at work and does not take kindly to change. He is articulate, has a good sense of humour and is usually very good with children.

Wood Goat: 1895, 1955

This Goat is generous, kind-hearted and always eager to please. He usually has a large circle of friends and involves himself in a wide variety of different activities. He has a very trusting nature but he can sometimes give in to the demands of others a little too easily and it would be in his own interests if he were to stand his ground a little more often. He is usually lucky in financial matters and, like the Water Goat, is very good with children.

Fire Goat: 1907, 1967

This Goat usually knows what he wants in life and he often uses his considerable charm and persuasive personality in order to achieve his aims. He can sometimes let his imagination run away with him and has a tendency to ignore matters which are not to his liking. He is rather extravagant in his spending and would do well to exercise a little more care when dealing with financial matters. He has a lively personality, many friends and loves attending parties and social occasions.

Earth Goat: 1919, 1979

This Goat has a very considerate and caring nature. He is particularly loyal to his family and friends and invariably creates a favourable impression wherever he goes. He is reliable and conscientious in his work but he finds it difficult to save and never likes to deprive himself of any little luxury which he might fancy. He has numerous interests and is often very well read. He usually gets much pleasure from following the activities of various members of his family.

PROSPECTS FOR THE GOAT IN 1997

The Chinese New Year starts on 7 February 1997. Until then, the old year, the Year of the Rat, is still making its presence felt.

The Year of the Rat (19 February 1996 to 6 February 1997) will have been a positive one for the Goat and he is likely to have accomplished much. In what remains of it, he should continue to set about his activities in a determined manner and follow up any opportunities he sees, particularly in his work. He should also advance any ideas that he has, especially of a creative or innovative nature, as he could find these favourably received. In the Rat year the Goat will find determined and positive effort on his part will be well rewarded and he should take every advantage of the positive aspects that prevail.

The Goat will also be fortunate in financial matters, although he would do well to keep a close watch over his level of spending, particularly as the latter part of the Rat year will be an expensive time for him. He could, however, enjoy several strokes of good fortune at this time and would do well to enter any competitions that catch his eye.

The Goat's domestic and social life will also be busy and while sometimes he may despair of all he has to do, there will nevertheless be pleasing times for him, too. Both his family and friends will bring him much pleasure as well as be a considerable source of pride to him. However, should he find himself under too much pressure or in need of advice, the Goat should not hesitate to ask for additional support or help. He will find both forthcoming.

The Goat would also do well at this time to try and complete any outstanding matters he has or tasks which he may have been putting off. Late November and the first week in December can be a most productive time for him and with a concerted effort he will be well pleased with what he is able to accomplish. However, despite his achievements, the Rat year will still have been a demanding one for him and as it draws to a close, the Goat should make sure that he gives himself the opportunity to relax and unwind and to enjoy himself over the Christmas and New Year holidays. After what he has accomplished over the last 12 months he has earned a well-deserved rest!

The Year of the Ox starts on 7 February and will be a challenging year for the Goat. He could find it difficult to make as much progress as he would like and could also have to deal with some problems which, while not serious, could take him some time to resolve. Ox years do not tend to be the easiest or smoothest of years for the Goat but provided he proceeds carefully and is not over-ambitious in his undertakings he can do much to minimize the more negative aspects that prevail.

In his work the Goat would do well to consolidate any recent gains he has made and take stock of his present position. He should continue to set about his duties in a conscientious manner and be prepared to adapt to new situations as they arise. He should also take careful note of all that is going on around him, in particular the views and opinions of his colleagues. This is also not a year when the Goat can afford to distance himself from events. To do so could leave him isolated and lacking support when he might need it. Also he should be wary about taking undue risks in his work or embarking on ambitious new projects without adequate preparation. This is very much a year for care.

However, despite the variable trends that exist, the Goat can, through hard and persistent work, make some progress. He will gain much useful experience and some of the problems he may face will turn out to be valuable learning opportunities. They will help him to review his objectives and learn from any mistakes he may have made, as well as do much to strengthen his resolve. The Goat himself knows he has many talents and some of what happens in 1997 will provide him with that extra impetus to make the most of himself. By giving of his best and by remaining determined he will slowly but surely begin to make headway, with the results of his efforts becoming apparent in the closing stages of the year and in 1998. Indeed, many have found that after facing events of a challenging nature there has followed a period of growth and achievement, and this will apply to the Goat in 1997. While the Ox year may not be easy, it will usher in a gradual but significant upturn in the Goat's fortunes.

Goats seeking work or a change in their present position should continue to follow up any openings that they see and, while not all their endeavours may meet with success, many will find their persistence rewarded. These Goats would also do well to consider types of work which they have not undertaken before. By doing so they could easily discover talents they did not know they possessed as well as usefully extend their experience. The months from September to December in particular could prove an active time for career matters and all Goats will generally find the second half of 1997 easier and a more productive time than the first.

The Goat does, however, need to exercise care when dealing with financial matters and particularly watch his level of spending. If he does get involved in any large transaction he should make sure he makes allowances for it in his outgoings and is fully aware of any obligations he might be placed under. This particularly involves property matters. If the Goat does have any uncertainties or doubts over any financial matter it would be in his interests to seek professional advice rather than take risks. He should also be wary of lending to others over the year and in all his financial dealings he does need to be vigilant.

Similarly, in his relations with those around him, the Goat needs to be his usual considerate self. In 1997 he should listen closely to others and remain mindful of their views and opinions. This is not a year when he can afford to be unduly stubborn or intransigent in his attitude; if he is, then the normally good relations he enjoys with so many could suffer. Fortunately, though, the Goat is usually adept in handling his personal relations and his skills in this area will help him do much to avert possible mis-understandings or difficult situations. However, should he find himself in any disagreement over the year he should seek a solution acceptable to all rather than ignore it or allow it to simmer in the background. With tact, discretion and his understanding nature, he can do much to minimize any awkward situations that do arise.

Despite the challenging nature of the Ox year, it will still contain some pleasurable times for the Goat. In particular his family life will give rise to some especially happy occasions and he will take much delight in following and encouraging the activities of those close to him. Also, some joint family activities, whether they concern household projects or more enjoyable pursuits such as outings or holidays, are likely to go well and give all concerned much pleasure.

The Goat's social life will also contain times of happiness and over the year he will attend several interesting and pleasant functions. He will also be able to extend his circle of friends quite extensively and any Goat who may be feeling lonely or seeking romance should aim to go out more and get in contact with others. He will find that effort on his part will bring pleasing results.

The Goat will also obtain much satisfaction from his hobbies, especially from any that allow him to use and expand upon his creative talents. If possible, he should try to contact those who share his interests as this will help further his knowledge as well as make his interest more fulfilling. The Goat will also carry out some improvements on both his home and garden over the year and while this may cause a period of disruption, he will be well pleased with the finished result. His fine artistic judgement will be as good as ever and projects involving interior decoration will give him – and those around him – much satisfaction.

However, in view of the testing nature of the year, the Goat should make sure that he gives himself a proper break over the year and, if possible, goes away for a holiday. He will find that a change of scene and break from his everyday routine will do much to refresh and revitalize him. He will also thoroughly enjoy any travelling that he undertakes during the year.

Although the Ox year will not be the easiest of years for the Goat, by being adaptable and careful in his activities he can do much to reduce some of the difficulties that present themselves. While his general level of progress may be modest rather than spectacular, all the time he will be adding to his experience and learning from the events, both good and bad, that occur. In many respects 1997 will be a year which allows him to reflect on his present position, sort out his priorities and strengthen his resolve. All this, and all that he learns, will hold him in good stead for the considerable opportunities that await him in the future. In this respect, 1997 is an important and necessary stepping-stone to the better times that lie ahead.

As far as the different types of Goat are concerned, 1997 will be a variable year for the *Metal Goat*. He may have to overcome some niggling problems which, while not serious, could prevent him from doing all he intended. In particular he could find some items of paperwork he has to complete particularly burdensome and may also find some of his undertakings are caught up in a welter of bureaucracy and form-filling. The Metal Goat needs to read any important document he has to complete or agreement he enters into through very carefully and make sure he understands all the implications. If he has any uncertainties he should check rather than take risks, particularly if there is finance involved. Similarly, if there is any matter concerning him or he has an important decision to take, he should not hesitate to seek the advice of others. The Metal Goat is in the fortunate position of having several around him who are keen to help and support him and for them to do this, he only has to ask. Throughout the year he will find much truth in the saying 'A worry shared is a worry halved.' However, while the Metal Goat will need to set about his activities with care, the year will still contain some pleasurable times for him. In particular, he can look forward to some pleasing news concerning a member of his family and a family event will also give him much joy – possibly a marriage, or the birth of a grandchild or even great-grandchild. In addition, the Metal Goat will take pleasure in some alterations that he carries out on his accommodation over the year. As usual his artistic talents and fine taste will be very much to the fore and some of the work he carries out will be much admired. His social life will also go well and he can look forward to attending several enjoyable parties and functions over the year. For Metal Goats who are seeking new friends, or who may have moved to a new area, it would really be in their interests to join local groups and get in contact with others. This could result in some new and meaningful friendships. Any travelling that the Metal Goat undertakes over the year is likely to go well, although to get the most from his travels and any holiday he takes he should read up about his destination before he leaves. This will make his visit all the more enjoyable for him. Generally, despite any problems that do arise over the year, there will be much that the Metal Goat will enjoy, and provided he is prepared to exercise care and patience with his undertakings, it can prove a reasonable and satisfying year for him.

This will be an interesting and varied year for the *Water Goat*. Early in 1997 he should give some thought to what he wishes to do over the year, whether in work, home improvements or some other sphere of his life. Then, with a plan in mind, he should work purposefully towards attaining his objectives. With careful planning and concentrated effort, he can achieve some creditable results. However, in all his undertakings the Water Goat should avoid taking unnecessary risks and will find he will obtain best results by concentrating on areas in which he has most experience. He should not be impatient for results or try to achieve too much too soon. Progress is possible but the Ox year is one which calls for some degree of patience! The Water Goat will also be helped by the supportive nature of those around him and if he has any doubts or uncertainties over the year he should not hesitate to seek the advice of others. He would also do well to keep alert to all that is happening around him and, when facing new and changing situations, should be prepared to adapt rather than show himself too resistant to change. He will find that some of the new situations in which he finds himself will lead to some interesting opportunities in the near future. He will also need to deal with any important correspondence and forms he receives with care; a delayed response on his part could cause problems later. Similarly, in matters of finance the Water Goat should not commit his money to any projects or transactions until he is satisfied with all the details. As with all Goats, this is not a year for taking undue risks. More positively, however, the Water Goat's personal interests will be of much benefit to him, especially any of a creative nature. If he finds he has some additional spare time at his disposal, he would do well to consider extending an existing hobby in some way, perhaps by writing about it or promoting his skills or knowledge. This way he could make the interest more fulfilling for him and pass many absorbing and happy hours. The Water Goat's domestic life is, however, likely to be busy over the year and there will be several family matters that will take up his time and attention. Some will be a source of much pleasure to him, especially as there will be good reason for a family celebration over the year, but some could cause him concern. If this is the case he should tell others of his feelings rather than keeping them to himself. Throughout the year he will find an open approach will do much to defuse any awkward situation that may arise and, as always, those around him will appreciate his warm, under-standing and well-meaning nature. Socially, too, this will be an active year and while the Water Goat can look forward to some enjoyable times with his friends he should not allow others to impose too much upon his good nature and find himself committed to undertakings he does not really want. Sometimes in 1997 it would be in his interests to stand firm and say 'No' to activities he has misgivings about. However, while 1997 may not be an entirely problem-free year for the Water Goat, providing he sets about his activities with care and uses his time efficiently, it can still prove a rewarding and fulfilling one for him.

This will be an important year for the *Wood Goat* and some of the action he takes and decisions he makes could have far-reaching consequences. Several events will take place over the year which will cause him to examine his current position, aims and objectives. As a result of his deliberations, he will decide to make some changes. Admittedly, the Wood Goat is not one who particularly relishes change and he may not enjoy some of the uncertainty that the year will bring, but he will find that the changes that occur will give him a renewed incentive to do well and make the most of himself. This is particularly so for any Wood Goat who may have felt staid or trapped in his present position. Many of the changes will concern the Wood Goat's work – some Wood Goats will transfer to a completely different position or take on duties they have never done before. What is asked of them may be daunting, but the Wood Goat has a rich fund of talents and by giving of his best will acquit himself well. In addition to the work changes, some Wood Goats will decide to move house. While this process will be time-consuming and at times frustrating, the Wood Goat will be pleased with his new accommodation and enjoy the changes and facilities that living in a new area will bring. Throughout the year he will also be helped by the support of his family and friends, and in times of uncertainty he should not hesitate to ask for assistance. His domestic life will, however, be generally busy over the year and there will be times when both he and his family members are tired or feel under pressure. At such times, it would be helpful for the Wood Goat to suggest some activities all could enjoy – perhaps a visit somewhere or local outing. For him, and others, to drive on relentlessly without an occasional break will only result in further tiredness and tension and possibly even lead to a straining of relations. All Wood Goats should be mindful of this. The Wood Goat should also make sure that he sets a regular time aside for his own interests, especially those that help him unwind and provide him with a break from his everyday activities. In this respect his interests and hobbies will prove highly beneficial for him, particularly those that might also give him some additional physical exercise. Generally, 1997 will be a demanding year for the Wood Goat and one which will contain several important changes. However, much of what occurs will help prepare him for the considerably better times that await him in the near future.

This will be a testing year for the *Fire Goat*. He can make reasonable progress in many of his activities, but in order for him to do so he must stay dedicated to his objectives. To make any sort of headway in 1997 will require discipline and effort on his part. Provided he is prepared to give of his best, however, he can do reasonably well. Furthermore, he will usefully extend his experience and impress those around him, both of which will help his progress in future years. In his work in particular, the Fire Goat needs to remain vigilant in his duties, avoid taking undue risks and be prepared to adapt to changing situations. This will be a demanding year and much will be asked of him, but provided he remains his determined and conscientious self, he can and will make progress. Those Fire Goats wanting to widen their experience or seeking employment should also make every effort to follow up any openings they see. Their persistence will be rewarded and while not every quest for promotion or work may be successful, a new position could develop in a most encouraging way. In many respects, what the Fire Goat accomplishes in 1997 will be preparing the way for the advances he will make in the future, particularly in 1998. The Fire Goat should also be careful in his financial undertakings and would do well to watch his general level of expenditure. This is not a year when he can afford to be too extravagant and if he does enter into any large transaction he should make sure he makes allowances for this in his budget. He should also be wary about committing himself to speculative ventures; all may not be as straightforward as it might at first appear. The Fire Goat's domestic life will be busy in 1997 and while there will be many demands made upon his time, his family will be a source of considerable pride to him. However, during the year he does need to remain mindful of the views of those around him and in case of any disagreement or awkward matter, he should seek a solution agreeable to all rather than remain intransigent or let the dispute linger on in the background. His family and friends will, however, provide him with much useful support over the year and the Fire Goat should listen closely to any advice he is given. Those around him do think highly of him and speak with his best interests at heart. He will also obtain considerable pleasure from outdoor activities and for those Fire Goats who enjoy gardening, walking or travelling or who are sporting enthusiasts, 1997 will contain some most enjoyable moments. Generally, this will be an active and, at times, demanding year for the Fire Goat but if he is prepared to make the most of himself and his abilities then he will make reasonable progress as well as do much to prepare the way for better things in years to come.

From a personal and social point of view 1997 will generally go well for the *Earth Goat*. Over the year he will be much in demand with those around him and there will be plenty of opportunities for meeting others, for making new friends and for romance. Some Earth Goats will get engaged and married over the year, although for those starting a new friendship, it may be best to let this develop gradually rather than rushing into a major commitment after just a short time. This way the friendship is more likely to be built on a securer foundation. In his personal relationships, however, the Earth Goat does need to listen closely to others and be mindful of their views and interests. He cannot expect to have things all his own way over the year and should any differences arise he should be prepared to compromise rather than remain inflexible. Domestically and socially, this can be a happy and pleasing year, but the Earth Goat does need to remain his usual considerate and understanding self. He will also have to assist and advise a more senior member of his family over the year and the help he is able to give will be highly valued. The Earth Goat will, however, need to exercise considerable care with financial matters in 1997 and if he enters into any large financial agreement he should make sure he understands all the terms and conditions he may be placed under. He should also not have to be too extravagant in his general level of spending – any savings that he eats into could be hard to replenish. The year will, however, contain some opportunities for the Earth Goat to progress in his work, although this may not always be easy. He may hold definite ideas about what he would like to do, but it may not be possible just yet for him to carry these out. He could be lacking the necessary experience or the openings could not yet be available. However, provided the Earth Goat is prepared to follow up any opportunities he sees and sets about his duties in his usual conscientious manner he will gain much valuable experience and this will stand him in good stead for the future. In work matters the Earth Goat needs to be adaptable, take up any openings offered to him and not hold so rigidly to his plans that he loses out on obtaining valuable experience. In future years he will make the progress he dreams of, but this is more a year for preparation and modest, rather than spectacular, advance. The Earth Goat could also find it advantageous to go on any courses for which he might be eligible or to try to add to his qualifications. Anything constructive he can do will certainly do much to enhance his prospects, especially late in 1997 and in 1998. Providing the Earth Goat sets about his activities with care this will be a useful year for him and personally it will contain times of much happiness.

FAMOUS GOATS

Pamela Anderson, Isaac Asimov, W. H. Auden, Jane Austen, Anne Bancroft, Boris Becker, Cilla Black, Ian Botham, Elkie Brooks, George Burns, Leslie Caron, John le Carré, Coco Chanel, Nat 'King' Cole, Harry Connick Jr, Angus Deayton, Catherine Deneuve, John Denver, Charles Dickens, Ken Dodd, Sir Arthur Conan Doyle, Umberto Eco, Douglas Fairbanks, Keith Floyd, Dame Margot Fonteyn, Anna Ford, Paul Gascoigne, Bill Gates, Mel Gibson, Newt Gingrich, Paul Michael Glaser, Mikhail Gorbachev, John Grisham, George Harrison, Sir Edmund Hillary, Hulk Hogan, John Humphrys, Isabelle Huppert, Billy Idol, Julio Iglesias, Mick Jagger, Paul Keating, Ben Kingsley, David Kossoff, Doris Lessing, Peter Lilley, Franz Liszt, John Major, Michelangelo, Joni Mitchell, Iris Murdoch, Rupert Murdoch, Mussolini, Randy Newman, Leonard Nimoy, Robert de Niro, Greg Norman, Oliver North, Des O'Connor, Lord Olivier, Michael Palin, Alain Prost, Keith Richards, Mickey Rourke, Sir Malcolm Sargent, Mike Smith, Freddie Starr, Lord Tebbit, Leslie Thomas, Lana Turner, Desmond Tutu, Mark Twain, Rudolph Valentino, Vangelis, Terry Venables, Lech Walesa, Barbara Walters, Andy Warhol, John Wayne, Tuesday Weld, Fay Weldon, Bruce Willis, Debra Winger, Tom Wolfe, Paul Young.

2 FEBRUARY 1908 ~ 21 JANUARY 1909	*Earth Monkey*
20 FEBRUARY 1920 ~ 7 FEBRUARY 1921	*Metal Monkey*
6 FEBRUARY 1932 ~ 25 JANUARY 1933	*Water Monkey*
25 JANUARY 1944 ~ 12 FEBRUARY 1945	*Wood Monkey*
12 FEBRUARY 1956 ~ 30 JANUARY 1957	*Fire Monkey*
30 JANUARY 1968 ~ 16 FEBRUARY 1969	*Earth Monkey*
16 FEBRUARY 1980 ~ 4 FEBRUARY 1981	*Metal Monkey*
4 FEBRUARY 1992 ~ 22 JANUARY 1993	*Water Monkey*

THE
MONKEY

THE PERSONALITY OF
THE MONKEY

Anything you're good at contributes to happiness.
       – Bertrand Russell: a Monkey

The Monkey is born under the sign of fantasy. He is imaginative, inquisitive and loves to keep an eye on everything that is going on around him. He is never backward in offering advice or trying to sort out the problems of others. He likes to be helpful and his advice is invariably sensible and reliable.

The Monkey is intelligent, well-read and always eager to learn. He has an extremely good memory and there are many Monkeys who have made particularly good linguists. The Monkey is also a convincing talker and enjoys taking part in discussions and debates. His friendly, self-assured manner can be very persuasive and he usually has little trouble in winning people round to his way of thinking – it is for this reason that the Monkey often excels in politics and public speaking. He is also particularly adept in PR work, teaching and any job which involves selling.

The Monkey can, however, be crafty, cunning and occasionally dishonest, and he will seize on any opportunity to make a quick gain or outsmart his opponents. He has so much charm and guile that people often don't realize what he is up to until it is too late. But despite his resourceful nature, the Monkey does run the risk of outsmarting even himself. He has so much confidence in his abilities that he rarely listens to advice or is prepared to accept help from anyone. He likes to help others but prefers to rely on his own judgement when dealing with his own affairs.

Another characteristic of the Monkey is that he is extremely good at solving problems and has a happy knack of extricating himself (and others) from the most hopeless of positions. He is the master of self-preservation.

With so many diverse talents the Monkey is able to make considerable sums of money, but he does like to enjoy life and will think nothing of spending his money on some exotic holiday or luxury which he has had his eye on. He can, however, become very envious if someone else has got what he wants.

The Monkey is an original thinker and, despite his love of company, he cherishes his independence. He has to have the freedom to act as he wants and any Monkey who feels hemmed in or bound by too many restrictions can soon become unhappy. Likewise, if anything becomes too boring or monotonous, he soon loses interest and turns his attention to something else. He lacks persistence and this can often hamper his progress. He is also easily distracted, a tendency which all Monkeys should try to overcome. The Monkey should concentrate on one thing at a time and by doing so will almost certainly achieve more in the long run.

The Monkey is a good organizer and, even though he may behave slightly erratically at times, he will invariably have some plan at the back of his mind. On the odd occasion when his plans do not quite work out, he is usually quite happy to shrug his shoulders and put it down to experience. He will rarely make the same mistake twice and throughout his life he will try his hand at many things.

The Monkey likes to impress and is rarely without followers or admirers. There are many who are attracted to him by his good looks, his sense of humour or simply because he instils so much confidence.

Monkeys usually marry young and for it to be a success their partner must allow them time to pursue their many interests and the opportunity to indulge in their love of travel. The Monkey has to have variety in his life and is especially well-suited to those born under the sociable and outgoing signs of the Rat, Dragon, Pig and Goat. The Ox, Rabbit, Snake and Dog will also be enchanted by the Monkey's resourceful and outgoing nature, but he is likely to exasperate the Rooster and Horse, and the Tiger will have little patience for his tricks. A relationship between two Monkeys will work well – they will understand each other and be able to assist each other in their various enterprises.

The female Monkey is intelligent, extremely observant and a shrewd judge of character. Her opinions and views are often highly valued, and, having such a persuasive nature, she invariably gets her own way. She has many interests and involves herself in a wide variety of activities. She pays great attention to her appearance, is an elegant dresser and likes to take particular care over her hair. She can also be a most caring and doting parent and will have many good and loyal friends.

Provided the Monkey can curb his desire to take part in all that is going on around him and concentrate on one thing at a time, he can usually achieve what he wants in life. Should he suffer any disappointments, he is bound to bounce back. The Monkey is a survivor and his life is usually both colourful and very eventful.

THE FIVE DIFFERENT TYPES OF MONKEY

In addition to the 12 signs of the Chinese zodiac, there are five elements and these have a strengthening or moderating influence on the sign. The effects of the five elements on the Monkey are described below, together with the years in which the elements were exercising their influence. Therefore all Monkeys born in 1920 and 1980 are Metal Monkeys, those born in 1932 and 1992 are Water Monkeys, and so on.

Metal Monkey: 1920, 1980
The Metal Monkey is very strong-willed. He sets about everything he does with a dogged determination and often prefers to work independently rather than with others. He is ambitious, wise and confident, and is certainly not afraid of hard work. He is very astute in financial matters and usually chooses his investments well. Despite his somewhat independent nature, the Metal Monkey enjoys attending parties and social occasions and is particularly warm and caring towards his loved ones.

Water Monkey: 1932, 1992

The Water Monkey is versatile, determined and perceptive. He also has more discipline than some of the other Monkeys and is prepared to work towards a certain goal rather than be distracted by something else. He is not always open about his true intentions and when questioned can be particularly evasive. He can be sensitive to criticism but also very persuasive and usually has little trouble in getting others to fall in with his plans. He has a very good understanding of human nature and relates well to others.

Wood Monkey: 1944

This Monkey is efficient, methodical and extremely conscientious. He is also highly imaginative and is always trying to capitalize on new ideas or learn new skills. Occasionally his enthusiasm can get the better of him and he can get very agitated when things do not quite work out as he had hoped. He does, however, have a very adventurous streak in him and is not afraid of taking risks. He also loves travel. He is usually held in great esteem by his friends and colleagues.

Fire Monkey: 1896, 1956

The Fire Monkey is intelligent, full of vitality and has no trouble in commanding the respect of others. He is imaginative and has wide interests, although sometimes these can distract him from more useful and profitable work. He is very competitive and always likes to be involved in everything that is going on. He can be stubborn if he does not get his own way and he sometimes tries to indoctrinate those who are less strong-willed than himself. The Fire Monkey is a lively character, popular with the opposite sex and extremely loyal to his partner.

Earth Monkey: 1908, 1968

The Earth Monkey tends to be studious and well-read, and can become quite distinguished in his chosen line of work. He is less outgoing than some of the other types of Monkey and prefers quieter and more solid pursuits. He has high principles, a very caring nature and can be most generous to those less fortunate than himself. He is usually successful in handling financial matters and can become very wealthy in old age. He has a calming influence on those around him and is respected and well liked by those he meets. He is, however, especially careful about whom he lets into his confidence.

PROSPECTS FOR THE MONKEY IN 1997

The Chinese New Year starts on 7 February 1997. Until then, the old year, the Year of the Rat, is still making its presence felt.

The Year of the Rat (19 February 1996 to 6 February 1997) is an auspicious year for the Monkey and in what remains of it he can accomplish much. Almost all areas of his life are well aspected but in order for him to take advantage of these favourable trends, the Monkey must resist the temptation of getting involved in too many activities all at the same time. In the Rat year he needs to concentrate on specific matters rather than spread his energies too widely.

In his work the Monkey can make considerable progress. His resourcefulness will be recognized and appreciated and he should actively advance any plans and ideas he has. If he sees any opportunity to make career advances he should also follow these up. The closing months of the Rat year can be a positive time for him and by acting in his usual enterprising manner he can do much to improve upon his present position.

The Monkey will also enjoy some good fortune in financial matters and would do well to consider setting aside some spare money for his longer term future. An investment he makes or savings scheme he starts in the Rat year could build into a useful asset in years to come.

Domestically and socially, the Rat year will also be generally most enjoyable and in what remains of it the Monkey can look forward to times of considerable happiness. The members of his family will be most supportive and give him much useful encouragement for his various endeavours. Although the Monkey tends to place great reliance upon his own judgement, he would do well to bear in mind any advice he is given, particularly in December 1996. By listening closely to others he will gain and learn much.

Socially, too, the end of the Rat year will be active and for any Monkey who has been feeling lonely or would like more friends, there will be several excellent opportunities to meet others in the months from October to December

1996. A friendship started towards the end of the Rat year could truly blossom in the Ox year. Romance and matters of the heart are especially well aspected at this time and all Monkeys will have good reason to enjoy the closing stages of the year.

Generally, the Rat year holds much potential for the Monkey and to get the most from this most favourable of years, it rests with him to use his time wisely and make the most of his wide and considerable talents.

The Year of the Ox starts on 7 February and will be a variable year for the Monkey. He can achieve a good level of progress with many of his activities but this is not a year when he can afford to be either complacent or take undue risks. The Ox, who rules the year, is a hard taskmaster and he expects the Monkey to give of his best and use his talents wisely rather than rest on his laurels. For the Monkey who is prepared to work and use his initiative, however, the rewards of the year can be significant.

In his work the Monkey would do well to consolidate any recent gains he has made or settle into any new position or responsibility he has been given. He should also continue to promote any new ideas he has as well as keep himself informed about all that is going on around him. This way he will be better placed to take advantage of any new situation that develops and, with his resourceful nature, he will indeed adapt well to most of the changes that take place over the year.

Monkeys who are seeking work or wanting a change from their present occupation should also remain persistent. Their determination will be rewarded and some Monkeys will be successful in obtaining a position with duties unlike anything they have done before. The Monkey will not only feel stimulated by the challenge this gives him but also discover talents he never appreciated he had. Indeed, many Monkeys will find that what happens in their work over the year will do much to test and develop their skills and this, in turn, will lead to an increased number of opportunities being available in the future.

The Ox year is also an ideal year for the Monkey to extend his skills and qualifications. If there is a subject he has been wanting to study this would be an excellent time to enrol on a course, whether at night school, by correspondence or personal study. Also, those Monkeys already involved in education are likely to do well and by applying themselves to their studies they will make pleasing progress. As all Monkeys will find in 1997, good results are possible from hard and determined work.

In his activities, however, the Monkey does need to co-operate with others and overcome his rather independent tendencies. Although he places much reliance on his own judgement and likes to do things in his own way, he will find better results will come from working in conjunction with others. Also, he would be helped if he were to set about his activities in a systematic and organized manner rather than leave everything to chance. This way he would achieve far better results and avoid the last minute rushes or periods of pressure that can so often arise from poor planning.

The Monkey will fare reasonably well in financial matters in 1997 but again a certain care is needed. The Monkey should keep a close watch on his level of expenditure and would do well to avoid risky or speculative ventures. If he has any doubts over any financial transaction he is about to enter into he would do well to check and, if need be, seek further advice. This is not a year for taking unnecessary risks. However, the Monkey could be helped by conducting a review of his financial position over the year; he could find he has several regular outgoings that are no longer necessary and by reducing these he could make some noticeable savings. The Monkey could also be fortunate in some purchases that he makes over the year both for himself and for his home. By remaining alert he could acquire some excellent bargains during sale times.

The Monkey is also likely to travel considerable distances in 1997 and while his travels will generally go well, it is important he checks the travel arrangements and connections carefully before he leaves. If not, he could find some journeys marred by missed connections or lengthy waits. Also, if he is visiting an area new to him, he could find it helpful to read up about it before he leaves. This way his visit will prove all the more meaningful. The Monkey should also take advantage of any opportunity he gets to visit friends or relations he has not seen for some time. Such visits will prove most pleasurable for all concerned.

The Monkey's domestic life will be busy and, at times, demanding and there will be several important matters that will require his attention. When dealing with domestic matters the Monkey should bear in mind the feelings and views of those around him rather than stick rigidly to his own ideas. Without a little give he could easily find differences and tensions arising and this is something he must strive to avoid. His domestic life can go well for him and prove most fulfilling, but care and forethought are needed. Also, if he himself has any worries or uncertainties, he should not hesitate to seek the views of those close to him. In many cases he will be reassured by the advice his loved ones give and, as always, be heartened by their support and encouragement. He could also find the occasional family trip or treat out will do much to help relations, particularly after busy and demanding times. The Monkey's family does mean much to him and in the Ox year it is important he devotes time and attention to his loved ones as well as listens carefully to their views.

Socially, too, 1997 will be an active year and many Monkeys will find that a friendship started in the Rat year will become significant. The Monkey can also look forward to attending some memorable parties and functions over the year and could well find himself the centre of attention at one of the functions he attends. The spring and summer months in particular will be a pleasing time for social matters, especially for the young and unattached Monkey.

Although many Monkeys pride themselves on keeping active and fit, the Monkey does need to take good care of himself over the year. If he relies heavily on convenience foods he could find switching to a more balanced and nutritious diet will do much to improve his energy levels and sense of well-being. Similarly, if he does not get much exercise during the day, he could find some additional physical activity of benefit. Without this extra care the Monkey could find himself lacking some of his usual zest and prone to minor ailments. The Ox year is not a year in which the Monkey can either neglect or ignore his well-being.

Generally, however, 1997 will be a reasonable year for

the Monkey although he does need to work hard and exercise a certain care with his activities. What he learns and accomplishes now will hold him in good stead for the future. In some respects, the Ox year is one in which the Monkey will be preparing himself for the more significant advances he will make in the future. It is also important, if he is to preserve the good relations he enjoys with so many, that he pays close attention to the views and feelings of others. If he bears this in mind, then the year will contain some thoroughly enjoyable times for him.

As far as the different types of Monkey are concerned, 1997 will be both a varied and interesting year for the *Metal Monkey*. During the year he will need to make some decisions concerning his longer term future. In this he should think carefully about all the options available to him and discuss his thoughts with those around him. The decisions he takes are likely to be the right ones, but he should resist taking any irrevocable action on the spur of the moment or against his better judgement. Time is on his side and with careful thought and deliberation the plans he makes will prove significant over the next few years. Throughout 1997 the Metal Monkey will also be helped by the supportive attitude of those round him and, if he is in a dilemma or has any uncertainties about any matter, he should not hesitate to avail himself of their advice. This will be a particularly important year for those Metal Monkeys in education and by applying themselves to their studies they are likely to attain some excellent results. Also, for Metal Monkeys not in education, it is an ideal year for them to add to their skills and they would do well to consider enrolling on a course which they feel may be useful. Academically, what the Metal Monkey achieves in 1997 is likely to hold him in good stead for the future. Also, any work experience that he obtains is likely to serve him well and, while his level of progress may not be as swift as he would like, what he does learn will prove of much value to him later. He will, however, need to watch his financial situation carefully over the year and try not to stretch his resources too far. Without care and sensible budgeting he could find himself having to dip into his savings and this could lead to problems later. This is not a year for undue extravagance or for taking financial risks. The Metal Monkey will, however, lead a pleasurable social life over the year and a friendship he made in the Rat year or makes in the first half of 1997 is likely to become important and long-lasting. The Metal Monkey will also obtain much enjoyment from outdoor activities over the year and from the travelling that he undertakes. However, before starting on any lengthy journey, he does need to sort out his travel arrangements and connections carefully before he leaves. Without this extra care, a missed connection or delay could mar some of his time away as well as lead to additional cost. Although the year will contain some uncertainties and his general level of progress may not always be as rapid as he would like, this can still be a pleasing time for the Metal Monkey. It will be a year for making plans, for adding to his skills and experience and, on a personal level, will also contain times of considerable happiness.

This will be a generally pleasant and fulfilling year for the *Water Monkey*. In 1997 he will have more time to devote to his interests and household projects than he has had recently and in this respect the year will prove most satisfying. Indeed, the Water Monkey would do well to consider extending one of his interests in some way – perhaps learning about a different aspect of it – or taking up a new hobby and something he has never done before. He will find this a stimulating challenge and one which will lead to many absorbing and fulfilling hours. It could also be worth his while to get in contact with others who share his interests, as this could help him to further his own knowledge and lead to some highly pleasurable social occasions. Any Water Monkey who may have experienced recent difficulties or is feeling lonely will find much comfort from joining a local club or society. In this respect, positive action on his part will lead to some pleasing results. The Water Monkey will also obtain much satisfaction from carrying out some projects on his home and garden over the year, although when using potentially dangerous pieces of equipment he should make sure he follows all the necessary safety precautions. Similarly, if he has to move heavy items he should seek assistance rather than risk straining himself. This is just not a year when he can afford to take risks with his personal safety or well-being. The Water Monkey also needs to deal with any important forms and paperwork he receives with care and if he has any doubts over what he is being asked he should check rather than guess or jump to conclusions. With-out this additional care, bureaucratic matters could prove troublesome and result in delays as well as waste a lot of his time. The Water Monkey could also be involved in several large transactions over the year, particularly involving improvements to his accommodation, and while he is usually astute in financial matters, it would be in his interests to check all the costs involved and watch his financial situation carefully. Without this vigilance, he could find himself involved in more expense than is necessary. Both domestically and socially the year will, however, hold some enjoyable times and he will take much pride in the achievements of those close to him. Also, although he may not wish to be viewed as interfering, any advice or assistance he feels able to give to family members and friends will be valued and much appreciated. His thoughtfulness and shrewd advice are always held in considerable esteem and this will be particularly the case in 1997. There will also be several opportunities for the Water Monkey to travel over the year and these trips will generally go well, especially if to destinations new to him. In addition, visits to local places of interest could also prove highly pleasurable. Generally, the Water Monkey will enjoy much of the year, particularly as he will be able to devote time and attention to activities that interest him. He does need to exercise care in bureaucratic and financial matters and when undertaking hazardous activities, but overall the year will turn out well for him.

The *Wood Monkey* has a keen and determined nature and usually a clear idea of the direction he is heading in. Providing he keeps his plans and objectives modest over the year he will make reasonable progress. He would, however, do well to stick to areas in which he has most experience and not take undue risks. This is a year for steady rather than rapid progress and he should refrain from being overly ambitious in his activities. Also, particularly in his work, the Wood Monkey needs to remain mindful of the views of those around him and show himself willing to adapt to changing situations. Although not all his plans may work out entirely in the manner he had hoped, what he does achieve will impress others and this will do much to help his future progress. Those Wood Monkeys seeking work or wanting to change their present position should remain vigilant and follow up any openings that they see. Their persistence will ultimately be rewarded and often in quite a surprising manner! The Wood Monkey will fare reasonably well in financial matters in the Ox year but should be conservative in his spending and avoid speculative undertakings. If he has any uncertainties over any financial matter it would be very much in his interests to check and seek further advice rather than take risks. The Wood Monkey's domestic life over the year is likely to be busy and there will be times when he will despair over the demands being made of him. However, at such times, he would find it helpful if he were to set himself some priorities rather than engage in too many separate undertakings, particularly household projects, all at one time. Also, if he feels under too much pressure, he should not hesitate to ask for additional help. The Wood Monkey is, after all, in the fortunate position of having others he can call on for support and assistance and this will be readily forthcoming should he ask. He may not be able to devote as much time to his social life and own interests as he would like, but it is still important that he allows himself the time to regularly unwind and gives himself a break from his everyday activities. He should also try to ensure that he goes away at least once over the year; he will find a change of scene most beneficial for him. Although 1997 will be a demanding year and he will have to work hard to make progress, what he does accomplish will do much to prepare the way for the more substantial gains and progress he will make in the future. This will be a busy but ultimately rewarding year, with the second half being more favourable and productive than the first.

This is a year which offers considerable potential for the *Fire Monkey*. In recent years he will have impressed others with his diligence and innovative manner and many Fire Monkeys will find their past labours rewarded with promotion, increased responsibilities or a new and more challenging position. Careerwise there are likely to be several positive changes taking place; however, these changes will put much pressure on the Fire Monkey and some of the things asked of him could prove daunting. This will be a year which brings both rewards and challenges. However, when the Fire Monkey does find himself under pressure he will be helped if he sets himself priorities and concentrates strictly on these rather than spreading his energies too widely. He will find one task well done is better than lots left half done. Also, what he accomplishes, as well as learns, over the year will do much to gain him the success he seeks. As far as financial matters are concerned, the Fire Monkey needs to keep a close watch on his general level of spending. With care he should not experience any serious problems, but this is still not a time when he can be over-indulgent or spend large sums without budgeting accordingly. The Fire Monkey's domestic life will, however, bring him considerable satisfaction. Although it will be busy, he can look forward to some pleasing times with those around him, especially over the spring and summer months, and will also find that his family members will support him well in his many activities. If he does have any uncertainties or feels in need of advice, he should not hesitate to seek their opinion; they do have his best interests at heart and he will find much reassurance and encouragement in the help he is given. In view of the active nature of the year the Fire Monkey may not have as much time for his social life as he would like. However, it is still important that he maintains regular contact with his many good friends and also allows himself time for his hobbies and interests. They do provide him with a valuable source of relaxation and this is especially valuable for him in view of the active nature of the year. He will obtain particular benefit from outdoor activities, especially from those that provide him with some additional exercise. Generally, 1997 will be a pleasing year for the Fire Monkey, but throughout it would be beneficial for him to set about his activities in an organized manner.

This will be a constructive and generally pleasing year for the *Earth Monkey*. He will be able to take stock of his present position and consolidate any recent gains he has made, particularly in his work. He will also find it a useful year to reflect upon his future aims and if he feels in need of further qualifications or skills he would do well to take action. All Earth Monkeys will greatly benefit from any additional study they undertake and, whether in employment or seeking employment, they would do well to enrol on any courses which they feel might be useful. What the Earth Monkey learns over the year will greatly assist his future progress and in some respects 1997 will be the year in which he will lay the foundation for the success that awaits him in later years. In addition to widening his experience, he should continue to set about his duties in his usual conscientious way and show himself adaptable in any new or changing situations in which he finds himself. He should also advance any ideas that he has – in 1997 he will do much to impress others, some of whom hold influence and can be of considerable help to him later. The months of October and November could prove particularly significant for career matters but generally the Earth Monkey should regard this more as a year for learning and preparation rather than for making the major advances he desires. Financial matters will generally go well for him during the year but he may face several large expenses, particularly concerning his accommodation and transport. When dealing with these, the Earth Monkey would do well to investigate all the options open to him and, if applicable, obtain prices and quotations from several different sources. This way he could save himself some significant outlay. He will enjoy the travelling he undertakes during the year and a holiday he takes in the summer months will be one of the most agreeable he has had for some years. The Earth Monkey's domestic life will be busy over the year and while there will be many demands on his time and numerous matters requiring his attention, those around him will be a source of much pride; in 1997 both his domestic and social life will afford him much pleasure. It is, however, important that the Earth Monkey does not neglect his own well-being over the year and if he does not get much exercise during the day he would do well to consider undertaking some additional physical activity such as walking, cycling or swimming. Generally, 1997 will be a satisfying year for the Earth Monkey and what he learns and accomplishes will stand him in good stead for the progress he will make in future years.

FAMOUS MONKEYS

Francesca Annis, Michael Aspel, Mike Atherton, Sue Barker, J. M. Barrie, David Bellamy, Jacqueline Bisset, Bjorn Borg, Victor Borge, Yul Brynner, Julius Caesar, Princess Caroline of Monaco, Johnny Cash, Chelsea Clinton, Joe Cocker, Colette, John Constable, Alistair Cooke, David Copperfield, Joan Crawford, Timothy Dalton, Bette Davis, Danny De Vito, Jonathan Dimbleby, Michael Douglas, Mia Farrow, Carrie Fisher, F. Scott Fitzgerald, Ian Fleming, Dick Francis, Fiona Fullerton, Arthur Hailey, Jerry Hall, Tom Hanks, Roy Hattersley, Stephen Hendry, Harry Houdini, Ray Illingworth, Tony Jacklin, P. D. James, Pope John Paul II, Lyndon B. Johnson, Edward Kennedy, Nigel Kennedy, Don King, Gladys Knight, Patti LaBelle, Leo McKern, Walter Matthau, Paul Merton, Princess Michael of Kent, Kylie Minogue, Martina Navratilova, Jack Nicklaus, Derek Nimmo, Peter O'Toole, Charlie Parker, Chris Patten, Anthony Perkins, Robert Powell, Mario Puzo, Debbie Reynolds, Tim Rice, Little Richard, Mary Robinson, Mickey Rooney, Diana Ross, Bertrand Russell, Paul Scofield, Tom Selleck, Omar Sharif, Wilbur Smith, Rod Stewart, Michaela Strachan, Jacques Tati, Elizabeth Taylor, Dame Kiri Te Kanawa, Harry Truman, Leonardo da Vinci, the Duchess of Windsor, Bobby Womack.

22 JANUARY 1909 ⁓ 9 FEBRUARY 1910	*Earth Rooster*
8 FEBRUARY 1921 ⁓ 27 JANUARY 1922	*Metal Rooster*
26 JANUARY 1933 ⁓ 13 FEBRUARY 1934	*Water Rooster*
13 FEBRUARY 1945 ⁓ 1 FEBRUARY 1946	*Wood Rooster*
31 JANUARY 1957 ⁓ 17 FEBRUARY 1958	*Fire Rooster*
17 FEBRUARY 1969 ⁓ 5 FEBRUARY 1970	*Earth Rooster*
5 FEBRUARY 1981 ⁓ 24 JANUARY 1982	*Metal Rooster*
23 JANUARY 1993 ⁓ 9 FEBRUARY 1994	*Water Rooster*

THE
ROOSTER

THE PERSONALITY OF
THE ROOSTER

Never put off for tomorrow what you can do today.
– Benjamin Franklin: a Rooster

The Rooster is born under the sign of candour. He has a flamboyant and colourful personality and is meticulous in all that he does. He is an excellent organizer and wherever possible likes to plan his various activities well in advance.

The Rooster is highly intelligent and usually very well read. He has a good sense of humour and is an effective and persuasive speaker. He loves discussion and enjoys taking part in any sort of debate. He has no hesitation in speaking his mind and is forthright in his views. He does, however, lack tact and can easily damage his reputation or cause offence by some thoughtless remark or action. The Rooster also has a very volatile nature and he should always try to avoid acting on the spur of the moment.

The Rooster is usually very dignified in his manner and conducts himself with an air of confidence and authority. He is adept at handling financial matters and, as with most things, he organizes his financial affairs with considerable skill. He chooses his investments well and is capable of achieving great wealth. Most Roosters save or use their money wisely, but there are a few who are the reverse and are notorious spendthrifts. Fortunately, the Rooster has great earning capacity and is rarely without sufficient funds to tide himself over.

Another characteristic of the Rooster is that he invariably carries a notebook or scraps of paper around with him. He is constantly writing himself reminders or noting down important facts lest he forgets – the Rooster cannot abide inefficiency and conducts all his activities in an orderly, precise and methodical manner.

The Rooster is usually very ambitious, but can be unrealistic in some of the things that he hopes to achieve. He occasionally lets his imagination run away with him and, while he does not like any interference in the things he does, it would be in his own interests if he were to listen to the views of others a little more often. He also does not like criticism and if he feels anybody is doubting his judgement or prying too closely into his affairs, he is certain to let his feelings be known. He can also be rather self-centred and stubborn over relatively trivial matters, but to compensate for this he is reliable, honest and trustworthy, and this is very much appreciated by all who come into contact with him.

Roosters born between the hours of five and seven (both at dawn and sundown) tend to be the most extrovert of their sign, but all Roosters like to lead an active social life and enjoy attending parties and big functions. The Rooster usually has a wide circle of friends and is able to build up influential contacts with remarkable ease. He often belongs to several clubs and societies and involves himself in a variety of different activities. He is particularly interested in the environment, humanitarian affairs and anything affecting the welfare of others. The Rooster has a very caring nature and will do much to help those less fortunate than himself.

He also gets much pleasure from gardening and, while he may not always spend as much time in the garden as he would like, his garden is invariably well-kept and extremely productive.

The Rooster is generally very distinguished in his appearance and, if his job permits, he will wear an official uniform with great pride and dignity. He is not averse to publicity and takes great delight in being the centre of attention. He often does well at PR work or any job which brings him into contact with the media. He also makes a very good teacher.

The female Rooster leads a varied and interesting life. She involves herself in many different activities and there are some who wonder how she can achieve so much. She often holds very strong views and, like her male counterpart, has no hesitation in speaking her mind or telling others how she thinks things should be done. She is supremely efficient and well-organized and her home is usually very neat and tidy. She has good taste in clothes and usually wears smart but very practical outfits.

The Rooster usually has a large family and as a parent takes a particularly active interest in the education of his children. He is very loyal to his partner and will find that he is especially well-suited to those born under the signs of the Snake, Horse, Ox and Dragon. Provided they do not interfere too much in the Rooster's various activities, the Rat, Tiger, Goat and Pig can also establish a good relationship with him, but two Roosters together are likely to squabble and irritate each other. The rather sensitive Rabbit will find the Rooster a bit too blunt for his liking, and the Rooster will quickly become exasperated by the ever-inquisitive and artful Monkey. He will also find it difficult to get on with the Dog.

If the Rooster can overcome his volatile nature and exercise more tact in some of the things that he says, he will go far in life. He is capable and talented and will invariably make a lasting – and usually favourable – impression almost everywhere he goes.

THE FIVE DIFFERENT TYPES
OF ROOSTER

In addition to the 12 signs of the Chinese zodiac, there are five elements and these have a strengthening or moderating influence on the sign. The effects of the five elements on the Rooster are described below, together with the years in which the elements were exercising their influence. Therefore all Roosters born in 1921 and 1981 are Metal Roosters, those born in 1933 and 1993 are Water Roosters, and so on.

Metal Rooster: 1921, 1981

The Metal Rooster is a hard and conscientious worker. He knows exactly what he wants in life and sets about everything he does in a positive and determined manner. He can at times appear abrasive and he would almost certainly do better if he were more willing to reach a compromise with others rather than hold so rigidly to his firmly held beliefs. He is very articulate and most astute when dealing with financial matters. He is loyal to his friends and often devotes much energy to working for the common good.

Water Rooster: 1933, 1993

This Rooster has a very persuasive manner and can easily gain the co-operation of others. He is intelligent, well-read and gets much enjoyment from taking part in discussions and debates. He has a seemingly inexhaustible amount of energy and is prepared to work long hours in order to secure what he wants. He can, however, waste much valuable time worrying over minor and inconsequential details. He is approachable, has a good sense of humour and is highly regarded by others.

Wood Rooster: 1945

The Wood Rooster is honest, reliable and often sets himself high standards. He is ambitious, but also more prepared to work in a team than some of the other types of Rooster. He usually succeeds in life but does have a tendency to get caught up in bureaucratic matters or attempt too many things all at the same time. He has wide interests, likes to travel and is very considerate and caring towards his family and friends.

Fire Rooster: 1897, 1957

This Rooster is extremely strong-willed. He has many

leadership qualities, is an excellent organizer and is most efficient in his work. Through sheer force of character he often secures his objectives, but he does have a tendency to be very forthright and not always consider the feelings of others. If the Fire Rooster can learn to be more tactful he can often succeed beyond his wildest dreams.

Earth Rooster: 1909, 1969

This Rooster has a deep and penetrating mind. He is extremely efficient, very perceptive and is particularly astute in business and financial matters. He is also persistent and once he has set himself an objective, he will rarely allow himself to be deflected from achieving his aim. The Earth Rooster works hard and is held in great esteem by his friends and colleagues. He usually gets much enjoyment from the arts and takes a keen interest in the activities of the various members of his family.

PROSPECTS FOR THE ROOSTER IN 1997

The Chinese New Year starts on 7 February 1997. Until then, the old year, the Year of the Rat, is still making its presence felt.

The Year of the Rat (19 February 1996 to 6 February 1997) will have been a challenging year for the Rooster and in what remains of it he will need to exercise care. In all his activities he should remain mindful of the views of others and, in any awkward situations, avoid being too intransigent. With the arrival of the Ox year, the aspects are about to swing in his favour and the last thing he should do is upset the normally sound relations that he enjoys with so many. The closing stages of the year call for tact, discretion and diplomacy.

In addition to exercising care in his relations with others, the Rooster also needs to watch his level of outgoings. The latter part of the Rat year could prove an expensive time for him and the Rooster must make sure that if he makes expensive purchases he budgets accordingly. He should also avoid buying on impulse and when involved in any large purchase would do well to check the various prices on offer rather than opt for the first one he sees. This way he could save himself some unnecessary outlay.

There will, however, be several opportunities for the Rooster to demonstrate his skills in his work at this time and his diligence and efficient manner will greatly impress others. By being co-operative and willing to adapt to new and sometimes demanding duties, he will do much to further his reputation and this will help his prospects in the new year. Also, Roosters seeking work should continue to follow up any opportunities that they see. From October 1996 the aspects will show a marked improvement and this will gather momentum as the Ox year approaches. The Rooster should also take advantage of any opportunity he gets to extend his experience and if there are any courses he thinks might be useful, he should follow these up. Anything he can do to enhance his skills now will be to his advantage as well as prove personally satisfying.

In view of the demands of the Rat year, the Rooster's domestic and social life may not always have gone as smoothly as he would have liked. In what remains of the year, he should make sure he devotes time and attention to those around him and should any tensions or difficulties exist, he should aim to resolve them. From a personal point of view, the closing months of the year will bring about an improvement in his relations with others and he can look forward to some enjoyable times with those around him. It is therefore an ideal time to make amends for any differences that might have occurred earlier in the Rat year.

As the year ends, the Rooster should give some thought to what he would like to accomplish over the next 12 months. Events will now move significantly in his favour and to take advantage of the improved trends he needs to have some idea of what he wishes to do next!

The Year of the Ox starts on 7 February and generally will be a settled and favourable year for the Rooster. Almost as soon as the Ox year begins he will begin to feel more positive in his outlook and will set about his activities with a greater enthusiasm. He will feel – with some justification – that the problems he has had to contend with of late are behind him and that this is a year in which he can look ahead with hope, optimism and a greater determination to make the most of himself and his abilities.

This determination on his part will, in turn, bring significant rewards in his work and almost all Roosters will improve on their position over the year. Throughout the Ox year the Rooster should actively advance any ideas he has. He will find these will be favourably received and indeed one idea or proposal he makes could have far greater consequences than he envisaged and will help his progress all the more. In the Ox year the Rooster will find much truth in the saying 'Nothing ventured, nothing gained' and if there is something he wishes to attain or promote he should act. There will also be several excellent opportunities for taking on new and more varied responsibilities and the Rooster should pursue any openings that he sees. The aspects for promotion and for transferring to a different position are excellent, especially in the first half of the year.

Those Roosters seeking employment should also remain committed to their quest for work. Their persistence will be rewarded and while some will obtain work in a different area from the one they seek, they could find that this will lead to other opportunities in the future. Generally, work matters will go well for the Rooster and most Roosters will take on more rewarding responsibilities as the year progresses. It is also a favourable year for those Roosters in education and by pursuing their studies in their usual dutiful way they will obtain some good results.

The Rooster will also enjoy an improvement in financial matters and any Rooster who may have experienced financial problems will find that these will ease as the year progresses. However, with this improvement, the Rooster would do well to put any spare money he has towards a specific purpose rather than spend it without too much thought. With travel well aspected, he could, for instance, consider spending some on a special holiday or, alternatively, in carrying out some home improvements that he may have been considering for some time. He could also enjoy good fortune in an investment that he makes over the year.

The Rooster's domestic life will be active and pleasurable

in 1997. Those around him will give him much useful encouragement and the Rooster would do well to listen to any advice that they give; they do speak with his best interests at heart. The Rooster should also make sure that he involves himself in the interests of those around him and resists the temptation of becoming so preoccupied with his own activities that he neglects those of others. Without a little care, this could result in some tensions and spoil an otherwise pleasing year. Also, in spite of his set ideas on how things should be done, the Rooster should aim to be a little more accommodating over the year. To be too inflexible and regimented in his activities and expect others to follow suit could result in some problems. This is again something the Rooster needs to watch.

Generally, however, his domestic life will go well and the year will contain many occasions which he and those around him will enjoy. These will not only include any outings and holidays that the Rooster arranges but also successes enjoyed both by himself and his relations. In 1997 there will be more than one occasion that will give rise to celebration! The Rooster's family means much to him and in 1997 he will be truly heartened by the love, support and encouragement those around him give.

Socially, the Rooster will find himself much in demand. He can look forward to attending several enjoyable functions over the year and will have every opportunity to extend his circle of friends and acquaintances. Any Rooster who may have been feeling lonely or had some sadness to bear should make every effort to go out more and get in contact with others. By making the effort he will enjoy a distinct upturn in his social life and can build up some new and meaningful friendships. The spring and early summer months will be an especially eventful time socially and for the unattached Rooster, the Ox year will bring some splendid opportunities for romance.

The Rooster will also find outdoor activities will go well and for those Roosters who are keen gardeners, sporting enthusiasts or travellers, the year will contain many truly pleasurable occasions. However, while he does usually keep himself in trim, the Rooster cannot afford to neglect his well-being. If he does not get much daily exercise, he should consider undertaking some additional walking or taking part in activities such as cycling or swimming; all could prove most beneficial for him. Also, if he is reliant on convenience foods, a more balanced diet could be to his advantage. In the Year of the Ox, it is particularly important that the Rooster takes good care of himself otherwise he could find himself lacking in energy and susceptible to minor ailments. Neither should he undertake risky activities without following the recommended safety precautions. As far as his personal safety and well-being is concerned, this is not a year for risks.

Another area in which the Rooster needs to exercise care is with paperwork and any important forms that he has to complete. He should check carefully all that is asked of him – a misinterpreted reply could take some time to resolve and involve him in some extra and onerous correspondence. Without extra vigilance on his part, bureaucratic problems could well occur and prove an unwelcome distraction.

Generally, however, the Ox year will be a positive year for the Rooster and by setting about his activities in his usual stout-hearted way he will make significant progress. Personally, too, the year will be most pleasurable and the Rooster can look forward to some happy and meaningful times with both his family and friends. He is blessed with many fine qualities and the Ox year will give him the chance to demonstrate his true worth.

As far as the different types of Rooster are concerned, 1997 will be an important and satisfying year for the *Metal Rooster*. To get the best from it he would do well to think about what he wishes to accomplish in the next 12 months and then, with some ideas in mind, he should earnestly set about achieving his objectives. Without any such plan, he could find himself drifting through the year and not making as much of himself or the opportunities that arise as he otherwise could. The plans that he draws up could concern almost anything – education matters, his interests, household projects or places that he would like to visit over the year – but to maximize the favourable trends that prevail the Metal Rooster does need to plan. Those Metal Roosters in education will have a particularly constructive year. Their studies will go well and their results will amply reward them for the time they have devoted to their work. Many of these Metal Roosters will also need to select subjects in which to specialize or choose new subjects to study. In this they need to decide carefully. They will choose well but it is not a decision they should rush and neither should they allow themselves to be persuaded into doing something against their better judgement. Some of the decisions they take will have a significant bearing on the next few years and could ultimately affect their choice of vocation. The Metal Rooster's domestic and social life will also go well and those around him will provide much useful support and encouragement. Should he have any problems or uncertainties, no matter what area of his life they might concern, he would be greatly helped if he were to speak of his concerns rather than keep them to himself. In turn, the Metal Rooster himself may have a relation who faces some difficult problem over the year and the attention and support he is able to give will be highly valued. The Metal Rooster will also obtain much satisfaction from his interests over the year, especially if he is able to join with others who can help further his knowledge. In addition, there will be several opportunities for him to travel in 1997 and while sometimes this may be at short notice, he will thoroughly enjoy the journeys he goes on and places he visits. Any Metal Rooster keen on improving his language skills would do well to take advantage of any opportunity to further them abroad. In most respects this will be a pleasurable and positive year and by using his time and skills well, the Metal Rooster can accomplish much.

This will be a year of change for the *Water Rooster* in almost any area of his life. Some changes will be planned, some not, but while they will give rise to moments of uncertainty and pressure, out of them will come new and brighter opportunities. In particular, many Water Roosters will see some significant changes in their daily activities. Some will transfer to new duties and be successful in obtaining a position they have been hankering after for some time while others will choose to retire. Some Water Roosters will also change their accommodation over the year and while the moving process could be protracted, they will delight in being in a new area, exploring the local environs and trying out the facilities on offer. However, those Water Roosters who do move – or, alternatively, undertake major household projects – should take extra care when lifting or moving heavy objects and using potentially dangerous tools. This is just not a year when the Water Rooster can take risks with his personal safety. Also, if he does feel tired or under par at any time, he should make sure he allows himself time to rest and recuperate rather than drive on relentlessly. The Water Rooster usually has a wide range of interests he can turn to which can help him relax and unwind. In particular he could find creative activities as well as those that take him out of doors both pleasurable and beneficial for him. The Water Rooster will also enjoy the travelling that he undertakes over the year, especially if it allows him to meet relations or friends he has not seen for some time. Financial matters will go well and many Water Roosters will receive an extra sum of money over the year, either for some work they have carried out in the past or from an unexpected source. In addition to his financial good fortune, the Water Rooster will also enjoy several strokes of luck in 1997 and would do well to enter any competitions that interest him. Although the year will contain some uncertainties and there will be times when he will feel under pressure, events will generally work out in his favour and herald a period of stability and contentment. Also, throughout the year, the Water Rooster should remember that he is in the fortunate position of having many around him he can call on for assistance and advice, and he should not hesitate to avail himself of this help should he need it.

In recent times, particularly in the Rat year, the *Wood Rooster* may have felt that he has not been making as much use of his talents and potential as he could or may have found the results he seeks elusive. The Ox year will, however, mark a significant improvement in his fortunes and his progress over the year will more than compensate for recent disappointments. However, to take advantage of these improved trends, he will need to set about his activities in a determined manner and use any opportunity he sees to promote himself and his talents. For the bold and enterprising Wood Rooster – and there are many! – the results of the year can be considerable. In his work the Wood Rooster can make great progress. Many Wood Roosters will find their past labours rewarded with promotion or increased responsibilities and those seeking work or a change from their present position could also enjoy some success. In addition, many Wood Roosters will find some skills that they learned some time ago will now prove valuable and that their wide-ranging talents will be in demand. The Wood Rooster should also advance any ideas that he has and, should he find himself in a changing situation, he should not resist the change but view it as heralding new opportunities for him. The Wood Rooster has an alert and sharp mind and over the year he will be given every chance to shine and make the most of his considerable abilities. He will also enjoy good fortune in financial matters and many Wood Roosters will take delight in redecorating and refurnishing their home or in purchasing some items for themselves which they have wanted for some time. Also, by remaining alert, the Wood

218

Rooster could acquire some splendid bargains over the year, sometimes in the most unexpected of places. Domestically, this will be a busy and eventful year. Many Wood Roosters will have good reason for a family celebration as well as take much delight in the achievements enjoyed by a younger relation. The Wood Rooster's social life, too, will go well and he can look forward to attending several enjoyable and memorable functions. Some of these will enable him to extend his circle of friends and acquaintances quite considerably and for the unattached Wood Rooster, one of these friendships could become truly significant. Generally, the Ox year holds much potential for the Wood Rooster and by promoting himself and pursuing the opportunities he sees he can make considerable progress. The aspects are favourable and it remains with him to take full advantage of them.

In recent years the *Fire Rooster* will have gained much valuable experience and, while he may not always have been able to make the progress he would have liked, he will now be able to put his experience to good use. In his work in particular, he can do especially well and most Fire Roosters will take on new duties as the year progresses. The Fire Rooster should actively pursue any opportunities he sees as well as promote his ideas; many think highly of his ambitious and diligent manner, and with the support and goodwill of those around him he will make significant progress. The months from April to July will prove especially positive for career matters. Fire Roosters who have suffered setbacks or adversity in recent years should regard 1997 as the year when they put the past behind them and focus their attention firmly on the present and the future.

With a bold and determined approach the Fire Rooster can accomplish much, and for many, their progress will be such that in the future they will come to view this year as one of the turning-points in their life. In addition to the progress the Fire Rooster will make in his work, he will also enjoy an improvement in his financial situation and many Fire Roosters will decide to go ahead with some household projects they have been contemplating for some time. With his fine taste and eye for detail, the Fire Rooster will be well-pleased with what he accomplishes. Also, if he has any spare money, he could consider investing it in a long-term savings plan – in future years it could build into a useful and valuable asset. There will also be several opportunities for the Fire Rooster to travel over the year and while sometimes this will be at short notice, he will greatly enjoy the journeys he makes and any holidays he takes. The Fire Rooster's domestic life will be busy and while there will be times when he will despair of all he has to do, those around him will be a source of much pride and happiness to him. They will also provide him with much valuable advice and encouragement and the Fire Rooster should pay great heed to their views and feelings. Overall, 1997 will be a positive year for him and will mark a distinct upturn in his fortunes. However, with the active nature of the year, the Fire Rooster does need to take good care of himself and make sure he keeps himself fit, eats and exercises well and gives himself the chance to regularly relax and unwind. To get the best from this most favourable of years he needs to be and stay on top form!

This will be a successful year for the *Earth Rooster* and he will to be able to make good progress with many of his activities. Furthermore, he will be given every opportunity to put his talents and the experience he has gained in recent years to good use. In his work he will greatly impress others and there will be opportunities for promotion or moving to newer and more varied responsibilities. For Earth Roosters seeking work or wanting to change their present position, the aspects are again encouraging. By remaining alert to all that is going on and pursuing the openings they see, they will be able to do much to improve upon their current situation. However, to make the most of these favourable trends the Earth Rooster should give of his best and show himself willing to adapt to new situations; sometimes he can be resistant to change, but to be too inflexible could hinder his progress. The Earth Rooster should also remain mindful of the views and opinions of those around him – again, too single-minded an attitude could undermine his progress. He will, however, enjoy an upturn in his financial situation over the year and an investment he makes or savings policy he starts now could work out well for him. He can also look forward to some pleasing times with his family and friends and many Earth Roosters will find themselves at the centre of a celebration. Personally, the year will hold several surprises! Those around the Earth Rooster will also provide him with much useful encouragement and should he have any uncertainties over the year he should not hesitate to seek their views. He will be reassured and heartened by much of the advice he is given. The Earth Rooster will also get much satisfaction from his interests, especially from any that provide him with additional exercise or take him out of doors. One of his interests could even prove lucrative for him and several times during the year the Earth Rooster will enjoy some strokes of good fortune. In most respects this will be a highly favourable year for him but there are two areas that could pose problems. The first concerns matters of a bureaucratic nature. The Earth Rooster does need to deal with important items of correspondence carefully and promptly; if not, he could find himself embroiled in a welter of additional paperwork and waste a lot of time when he could be more usefully occupied. Secondly, he needs to tackle his activities at a sensible pace rather than drive himself relentlessly or put himself under unnecessary pressure. Without care, he could find himself becoming tired, tense and certainly not making as much of himself or the year as he could. In 1997 the Earth Rooster will make progress but it is important, too, that he enjoys the year and regularly relaxes and unwinds. Generally, though, the Ox year is one which offers considerable scope to the Earth Rooster and in which he can make excellent progress.

FAMOUS ROOSTERS

Adamski, Kate Adie, Danny Baker, Dame Janet Baker, Severiano Ballesteros, Sir Dirk Bogarde, Richard Briers, Michael Caine, Jasper Carrott, Enrico Caruso, Charles Cazenove, Jean Chrétien, Eric Clapton, Joan Collins, Rita Coolidge, Steve Davis, Cathy Dennis, Sasha Distel, the Duke of Edinburgh, Ernie Els, Gloria Estefan, Nick Faldo, Bryan Ferry, Errol Flynn, Benjamin Franklin, Dawn French, Stephen Fry, David Gower, Steffi Graf, Melanie Griffith, Richard Harris, Deborah Harry, Goldie Hawn, Katherine Hepburn, Michael Heseltine, Alain Juppé, Diane Keaton, Nancy Kerrigan, Larry King, Dean Koontz, Bernhard Langer, Brian Lara, D. H. Lawrence, Martyn Lewis, David Livingstone, Ken Livingstone, Jayne Mansfield, Steve Martin, James Mason, W. Somerset Maugham, Bette Middler, Van Morrison, Willie Nelson, Paul Nicholas, Barry Norman, Kim Novak, Yoko Ono, Donny Osmond, Dolly Parton, Michelle Pfeiffer, Nancy Reagan, Joan Rivers, Paul Scofield, Jenny Seagrove, Sir Harry Secombe, George Segal, Carly Simon, Johann Strauss, Barbara Taylor Bradford, Jayne Torvill, Sir Peter Ustinov, Richard Wagner, Neil Young.

10 FEBRUARY 1910 ~ 29 JANUARY 1911		*Metal Dog*
28 JANUARY 1922 ~ 15 FEBRUARY 1923		*Water Dog*
14 FEBRUARY 1934 ~ 3 FEBRUARY 1935		*Wood Dog*
2 FEBRUARY 1946 ~ 21 JANUARY 1947		*Fire Dog*
18 FEBRUARY 1958 ~ 7 FEBRUARY 1959		*Earth Dog*
6 FEBRUARY 1970 ~ 26 JANUARY 1971		*Metal Dog*
25 JANUARY 1982 ~ 12 FEBRUARY 1983		*Water Dog*
10 FEBRUARY 1994 ~ 30 JANUARY 1995		*Wood Dog*

THE
DOG

THE PERSONALITY OF THE DOG

It is no use saying, 'We are doing our best.' You have to succeed in doing what is necessary.
                                    – *Sir Winston Churchill: a Dog*

The Dog is born under the signs of loyalty and anxiety. He usually holds very firm views and beliefs and is the champion of good causes. He hates any sort of injustice or unfair treatment and will do all in his power to help those less fortunate than himself. He has a strong sense of fair play and will be honourable and open in all his dealings.

The Dog is very direct and straightforward. He is never one to skirt round issues and speaks frankly and to the point. He can also be stubborn, but he is more than prepared to listen to the views of others and will try to be as fair as possible in coming to his decisions. He will readily give advice where it is needed and will be the first to offer assistance when things go wrong.

The Dog instils confidence wherever he goes and there are many who admire him for his integrity and resolute manner. He is a very good judge of character and he can often form an accurate impression of someone very shortly after meeting them. He is also very intuitive and can frequently sense how things are going to work out long in advance.

Despite his friendly and amiable manner, the Dog is not a big socializer. He dislikes having to attend large social functions or parties and much prefers a quiet meal with friends or a chat by the fire. The Dog is an excellent conversationalist and is often a marvellous raconteur of amusing stories and anecdotes. He is also quick-witted and his mind is always alert.

He can keep calm in a crisis and although he does have a temper, his outbursts tend to be short-lived. The Dog is loyal and trustworthy, but if he ever feels badly let down or rejected by someone, he will rarely forgive or forget.

The Dog usually has very set interests. He prefers to specialize and become an expert in a chosen area rather than dabble in a variety of different activities. He usually does well in jobs where he feels that he is being of service to others and is often suited to careers in the social services, the medical and legal professions and teaching. The Dog does, however, need to feel motivated in his work. He has to have a sense of purpose in the things that he does and if ever this is lacking he can quite often drift through life without ever achieving very much. Once he has the motivation, however, very little can prevent him from securing his objective.

Another characteristic of the Dog is his tendency to worry and to view things rather pessimistically. Quite often these worries are totally unnecessary and are of his own making. Although it may be difficult, worrying is a habit which the Dog should try to overcome.

The Dog is not materialistic or particularly bothered about accumulating great wealth. As long as he has the necessary money to support his family and to spend on the occasional luxury, he is more than happy. However, when he does have any spare money he tends to be rather a spendthrift and does not always put his money to its best use. He is also not a very good speculator and would be advised to get professional advice before entering into any major long-term investment or commitment.

The Dog will rarely be short of admirers, but he is not an easy person to live with. His moods are changeable and his standards high, but he will be loyal and protective to his partner and will do all in his power to provide her with a good and comfortable home. He can get on extremely well with those born under the signs of the Horse, Pig, Tiger and Monkey, and can also establish a sound and stable relationship with the Rat, Ox, Rabbit, Snake and another Dog, but will find the Dragon a bit too flamboyant for his liking. He will also find it difficult to understand the creative and imaginative Goat and is likely to be highly irritated by the candid Rooster.

The female Dog is renowned for her beauty. She has a warm and caring nature, although until she knows someone well she can be both secretive and very guarded. She is highly intelligent and despite her calm and tranquil appearance she can be extremely ambitious. She enjoys sport and other outdoor activities and has a happy knack of finding bargains in the most unlikely of places. She can also get rather impatient when things do not work out as she would like.

The Dog usually has a very good way with children and can be a loving and doting parent.

He will rarely be happier than when he is helping someone or doing something that will benefit others. Providing he can cure himself of his tendency to worry, he will lead a very full and active life – and in that life he will make many friends and do a tremendous amount of good.

THE FIVE DIFFERENT TYPES OF DOG

In addition to the 12 signs of the Chinese zodiac, there are five elements and these have a strengthening or moderating influence on the sign. The effects of the five elements on the Dog are described below, together with the years in which the elements were exercising their influence. Therefore all Dogs born in 1910 and 1970 are Metal Dogs, those born in 1922 and 1982 are Water Dogs, and so on.

Metal Dog: 1910, 1970

The Metal Dog is bold, confident and forthright, and sets about everything he does in a resolute and determined manner. He has a great belief in his abilities and has no hesitation about speaking his mind or devoting himself to some just cause. He can be rather serious at times and can get anxious and irritable when things are not going according to plan. He tends to have very specific interests and it would certainly help him to broaden his outlook and also become more involved in group activities. He is extremely loyal and faithful to his friends.

Water Dog: 1922, 1982

The Water Dog has a very direct and outgoing personality. He is an excellent communicator and has little trouble in persuading others to fall in with his plans. He does, however, have a somewhat carefree nature and is not as disciplined or as thorough as he should be in certain matters. Neither does he keep as much control over his finances as he should, but he can be most generous to his family and friends and will make sure that they want for nothing. The Water Dog is usually very good with children and has a wide circle of friends.

Wood Dog: 1934, 1994

This Dog is a hard and conscientious worker and will usually make a favourable impression wherever he goes. He is less independent than some of the other types of Dog and prefers to work in a group rather than on his own. He is popular, has a good sense of humour and takes a very keen interest in the activities of the various members of his family. He is often attracted to the finer things in life and can get much pleasure from collecting stamps, coins, pictures or antiques. He also prefers to live in the country rather than the town.

Fire Dog: 1946

This Dog has a lively, outgoing personality and is able to establish friendships with remarkable ease. He is an honest and conscientious worker and likes to take an active part in all that is going on around him. He also likes to explore new ideas, and providing he can get the necessary support and advice, he can often succeed where others have failed. He does, however, have a tendency to be stubborn. Providing he can overcome this, the Fire Dog can often achieve considerable fame and fortune.

Earth Dog: 1898, 1958

The Earth Dog is very talented and astute. He is methodical and efficient and is capable of going far in his chosen profession. He tends to be rather quiet and reserved but has a very persuasive manner and usually secures his objectives without too much opposition. He is generous and kind and is always ready to lend a helping hand when it is needed. He is also held in very high esteem by his friends and colleagues and he is usually most dignified in his appearance.

PROSPECTS FOR THE DOG IN 1997

The Chinese New Year starts on 7 February 1997. Until then, the old year, the Year of the Rat, is still making its presence felt.

The Year of the Rat (19 February 1996 to 6 February 1997) will have been a pleasing year for the Dog and the closing stages will be a fulfilling and generally positive time for him. However, to take advantage of the trends that prevail, the Dog should take careful note of all that is happening around him as well as be prepared to act in close co-operation with others. This is just not a time when he can be too independent in his actions or distance himself from what is going on. By remaining vigilant and keeping himself well-informed, he could receive some information, learn of an opportunity or meet someone with influence, any of which will be to his advantage.

In his work, the Dog will have done much to impress others and many Dogs will have found their efforts and

YOUR CHINESE HOROSCOPE 1997

loyalty rewarded in some way. This could have been by a
salary increase, a special award or being given additional
duties. In what remains of the Rat year, the Dog will
continue to do well and his efforts will be much appreciated. Those Dogs seeking work will also have some encouraging news in the latter part of the year and should
continue to pursue any opportunities they see. The Dog
does possess a tenacious streak and his persistence will, in
time, pay off.

The Dog will also fare well in financial matters, although
it would be in his interests to keep a watchful eye on his
level of spending. December will be an expensive month
for him and he does need to make allowances for the extra
outlay he makes. He will, however, be fortunate in some
purchases he makes in the post-Christmas sales and would
do well to keep alert for bargains, both for himself and his
home, at this time.

The Dog's domestic life will also bring him much satisfaction and he can look forward to some pleasing times
with those around him. Again, joint activities are favoured
and the Dog would do well to involve those around him in
all that he does. He can also look forward to attending
several enjoyable social events towards the end of the Rat
year and for any Dog who may be feeling lonely or in need
of friends it really would be in his interests to go out more
and get in contact with others. Positive action on his part
will bring results and by making the effort the latter part
of the Rat year can be a truly happy time for him.

In the closing stages of the Rat year the Dog must assert
himself and use his talents to the fullest. For the bold and
determined Dog this can be a most favourable time.

The Year of the Ox starts on 7 February and will be a mixed year for the Dog. He could find that his progress is slow and that it is not possible to accomplish all he would like. However, despite the variable trends, the year will still hold some pleasant times for him as well as being quite constructive.

In 1997 the Dog would do well to concentrate his energies on areas in which he has most experience rather than embark on ambitious new ventures. Neither should he start on any major project without adequate preparation or making sure he enjoys the support of others. The Ox year is not a year in which he can take undue risks or act too independently of others.

In his work the Dog would do well to consolidate any recent gains he has made. Those around him think highly of him and by continuing to set about his duties in his usual conscientious manner, the Dog will be able to make steady if not exactly swift progress. However, should he be asked to introduce changes in his duties he should show himself willing to adapt and be prepared to learn new techniques and procedures. Sometimes the Dog can be reluctant to change and too inflexible an attitude could undermine some of the goodwill he has established. Also the Dog will find that by adapting to change, new opportunities could emerge which will be to his longer term advantage. In addition, he needs to take careful note of the views and opinions of his colleagues and bear these in mind with any ideas or plans that he has. Throughout the year he will find progress so much easier by joining forces and co-operating with others rather than going his own way. Also, should he find himself in a fraught or difficult situation, he needs to remain diplomatic and tactful, other-wise he could end up saying things he might later regret. As far as his relations with his colleagues are concerned, 1997 is a year for tact, care and a willingness to co-operate.

The Dog would greatly benefit from extending his skills over the year and he should take advantage of any oppor-tunity to attend courses or widen his experience in some way. If there is a subject that has been interesting him or he has been intending to study, this would be an excellent year to start. It is also a favourable year for those Dogs in education and by applying themselves to their studies they will obtain some pleasing results and be well rewarded for the time and sacrifices they have had to make.

Dogs seeking work should actively follow up any open-ings that they see. They could find their efforts rewarded in a most surprising way – either by hearing of an oppor-tunity by chance or being offered something they have never done before and which they will, in time, find they are ideally suited for. Their endeavours to find work may not always be easy, but their tenacity will ultimately produce results. Generally, all Dogs will find the second half of the year more favourable for employment matters than the first and there will be a distinct upturn in their fortunes from September onwards. This upturn will gather pace as 1998 approaches and will continue through the more favourable Tiger year.

The Dog will fare reasonably well in financial matters although he could face several large expenses over the year, particularly connected with his accommodation and trans-port. When this occurs – and, indeed, when facing any large expenditure – the Dog needs to go into the matter extremely carefully. If he has to arrange for any work to be carried out, it would be worth him obtaining several quotations rather than opting for the first one he is given. This is not a year when he can take risks or be too complacent when dealing with financial matters. Also, he should be particularly wary of any speculative schemes that he may hear about – all is not as straightforward as it might seem and without care he could find himself losing money. Similarly, he should avoid lending to others, as he could experience problems in getting his money back.

The Dog will, however, take great pride in the progress and successes enjoyed by family members in 1997 and the support and encouragement he is able to give will be truly valued. There will also be good reason for him to be involved in a family celebration over the year and the summer months in particular are likely to be a content and fulfilling time. However, throughout the Ox year, the Dog does need to remain mindful of the opinions of those close to him and when he has any uncertainties or decisions to make he should pay great heed to the advice he is given. Those around him do have his best interests at heart and he should listen carefully to all he is told.

Generally, domestic matters can go well in 1997, but should any differences arise, the Dog should aim to sort these out as quickly and amicably as he can. To let differences linger in the background could take the edge off some pleasurable occasions. Also, throughout the year, he needs to remain tactful in what he says. To be too blunt or forthright could result in some acrimonious exchanges and hurt feelings. Dogs, be warned! This same care extends to the Dog's social life. A friendship or an event he attends could easily be jeopardized by a thoughtless remark or difference of opinion. This is very much a year for diplomacy. However, if the Dog bears this in mind, his social life will provide him with much pleasure and again the summer months will prove a favourable time. Dogs seeking new friends or romance will find the months from June to August especially happy and a friendship formed during the summer could become significant and long-lasting.

With the demands of the year it is also important that the Dog does not neglect his own interests and he should aim to set a regular time aside to devote to his hobbies and recreational pursuits. They do provide him with an important source of relaxation and in view of some of the pressures he may find himself under, it is essential that he gives himself the opportunity to regularly rest and unwind. Although travel may not figure too prominently over the year it is also important that the Dog tries to go away for a holiday or has a proper break. He will find a change of scene most beneficial for him.

Although the Ox year may not be without its problems, provided the Dog keeps his expectations modest and exercises care in his relations with others, he will do much to negate some of the more difficult aspects that prevail. Anything he can do to further his skills and abilities will be to his future advantage, especially with the upturn in his fortunes which will come in the latter part of the Ox year and gather momentum as the Tiger year approaches.

As far as the different types of Dog are concerned, the Year of the Ox may not be the smoothest of years for the *Metal*

Dog but it will nevertheless be a valuable one. In spite of his efforts, he could find that he is not making as much progress as he would like and that he has to look again at some of his longer term objectives. While the year will contain its uncertainties and a few disappointments, this period of reflection and self-examination will prove most helpful to him. In particular it will enable him to focus upon new objectives and give him an incentive to make more of himself and realize his potential. Also, for those Metal Dogs who may have been feeling staid or in a rut, the events of the year will give them an added impetus to improve and advance upon their present position. For many Metal Dogs, 1997 will be a year for making significant plans that they will be able to put into operation in the closing stages of the Ox year and in the more favourable Tiger year. However, in 1997, the Metal Dog should avoid taking any precipitous action without making sure he enjoys the backing and support of others. As far as his work is concerned, he needs to set about his activities cautiously and remain mindful of the events going on around him and the views of his colleagues. This is just not a year when he can be too independent in his attitude or distance himself from events. He should also be prepared to adapt to changing situations. While he may have misgivings about some of what is taking place, too inflexible an attitude could undermine his position. In his work, care and tact are very much needed. Metal Dogs seeking work could find their efforts rewarded in quite an unexpected way and that one position they obtain will lead to considerably better opportunities in the near future. The Metal Dog does, however, need to keep a close watch on his level of spending and he could find it of particular help to review his regular outgoings. He could find some of these are no longer necessary and a few modifications will result in some savings. His domestic life, although busy, will bring him much pleasure and he will take considerable satisfaction in the achievements of a younger relation. The Metal Dog would, however, do well to involve his family in his various activities and in times of uncertainty, he should seek their views and assistance. To keep his worries or concerns to himself could put him under increased pressure when, in effect, those around him are more than willing to provide support and advice. Generally, in 1997 the Metal Dog needs to set about his activities with care and give thought to his future aspirations. What he plans and achieves in the Ox year will have far-reaching consequences and be the prelude for the more successful and progressive times that are about to enter his life.

The Year of the Ox will be a busy year for the *Water Dog* and there will be times when he will find himself under pressure or have important decisions to make concerning his future. However, provided he tackles his activities in an efficient manner and is prepared to seek the advice of others when facing decisions, he will do much to ease some of the pressures and dilemmas he might find himself under. The Water Dog is in the fortunate position of having many he can turn to for advice and throughout the year he should not hesitate to do so. His family, in particular, will give him much useful assistance and he would do well to involve them in his activities. During the year he will find those around him will put his mind at ease on more than one occasion as well as relieve some of the pressure that he might be under. This also applies to those Water Dogs in education. Those around them are keen to see that they make the most of their potential and they should be open about any difficulties they have with their studies and listen carefully to the advice they are given, especially by those more senior to them, who speak with experience. The one thing all Water Dogs should guard against is bottling up their feelings and anxieties; to do so could only make matters worse and in some cases they could even find they are worrying themselves unnecessarily. The Water Dogs in education will, however, make satisfying progress over the year, although they should set about their studies in an organized and systematic way. To leave revision or work on projects to the last minute could cause a lot of unnecessary pressure (and panic!) as well as lead to less satisfactory results. In 1997 they should aim to work consistently and at all times give of their best. Also what they learn over the year will be of considerable help to them in the future and in some cases, could influence their choice of future vocation. All Water Dogs will get much pleasure from their social life over the year and can look forward to having some enjoyable times with their friends. However, as with all other Dogs, the Water Dog does need to stay mindful of the views and interests of those around him and, in the case of a difference of opinion arising, exercise tact in what he says. He will get much enjoyment from outdoor activities in 1997 and for those Water Dogs who engage in or follow sport the year will contain some truly satisfying moments. The Water Dog does, however, need to keep a watchful eye on his expenses over the year and should avoid stretching his resources too far. Although the Ox year will at times be demanding for him, it need not be an adverse year. Provided he sets about his activities sensibly and seeks advice at important times he will make steady progress. While the year will be busy, it will still contain some happy and rewarding times, with the period from June to August being particularly favourable.

This will be a generally satisfying year for the *Wood Dog*, although he will need to exercise care with some of his activities. On the positive side, his domestic and social life will generally prove pleasurable and he will take much delight in following the activities of those close to him. However, throughout 1997, he does need to stay mindful of their views and feelings and while he may hold set ideas on how he likes things to be done, if he meets with any opposition he should be prepared to be flexible rather than intransigent. To be unduly stubborn, especially over a relatively small matter, could lead to some ill-feeling and spoil an otherwise pleasing year. This is something all Wood Dogs should bear in mind. The Wood Dog will, however, delight in the time that he devotes to his interests and hobbies over the year and these will provide him with many satisfying moments. Anything that he can do to further his interests, either by getting in contact with fellow enthusiasts or learning about another aspect of his interest, will make it all the more fulfilling. The Wood Dog will also find outdoor activities will go especially well and for those who enjoy visiting places of local interest, exploring the countryside, gardening or sport, the year will contain some truly splendid moments. Many Wood Dogs will also carry out some work on their accommodation over the year and in this care is needed. The Wood Dog should be especially careful if he has to move any cumbersome objects, as a strain could cause him prolonged discomfort. He should also make sure he follows safety precautions when undertaking any hazardous task or using potentially dangerous equipment. If he has any doubts or concerns about a task he is about to tackle, he should make sure he gets assistance and, if need be, further advice. This is just not a year when he can take risks with his personal safety or well-being. The Wood Dog may also encounter some problems of a bureaucratic nature over the year and should deal with any important forms and items of correspondence with care. Again, if he has any doubts, he should check rather than take risks or jump to conclusions. He may not travel too far over the year although any breaks and holidays that he takes will go well and prove beneficial for him. Wood Dogs who may be feeling lonely should also make every effort to go out more and get in contact with others. Socially, this can be a pleasing year, but if the Wood Dog is seeking new friends, he must make that all-important initial effort. Although he may experience some problems in 1997, these are more likely to be nigglesome than serious and overall will not prevent him from enjoying much of the year.

The *Fire Dog* is determined, direct and bold, and while these qualities have served him well over the years, in 1997 he must exercise a certain restraint in his undertakings. This is not a year when he can set about ambitious new projects or go about his activities without the support and backing of others. Neither is it one in which he can get involved in risky undertakings. In all that he does he needs to remain mindful of the views of those around him and take into consideration the prevailing situation. Sometimes the Fire Dog is tempted to proceed with his ideas regardless; to do so in the Ox year could leave him isolated and undermine his position. However, while the Fire Dog could feel frustrated by the restraining influence of the Ox year, he can still obtain much of value from it. Some of the events – including some of the niggling bureaucratic problems he may encounter – will cause him to reflect upon his present situation, his future aspirations and how he would like to see his life developing over the next few years. The ideas he develops will prove immensely helpful to him in the future, so much so that some Fire Dogs will come to regard 1997 as the closing chapter of one part of their life, with 1998 and subsequent years heralding change and exciting new challenges. However, over the present year, the Fire Dog should keep his immediate plans modest and be prepared to discuss his thoughts and ideas with those around him. By doing so he will obtain much useful and pertinent advice. As far as his work is concerned, he will need to proceed with care and if he finds himself in a new or changing situation he should adapt rather than adopt too inflexible an attitude. To run contrary to the views of those around him could undermine some of the goodwill he has built up. The Fire Dog would also do well to watch his level of spending over the year as without care this could be greater than he thought. Both domestically and socially, however, it will be a generally pleasing year for him and he can look forward to some special and memorable times with those close to him. He should, though, make every effort to involve others in his activities and when he faces uncertainties or difficult decisions he should seek their views rather than brood over the matter alone. Those around him hold him in great esteem and he should avail himself of the support and encouragement they can offer. This may not always be an easy year for the Fire Dog and he will have to exercise care in his activities, but if he views the Ox year as one for taking stock of his present situation and for planning for the future, then it will turn out to be a significant year for him.

This will be a reasonable year for the *Earth Dog* and while his level of progress may not be as great as he would like, he can still gain much from it. In his work he will be able to consolidate any recent gains he has made and by continuing to set about his activities in his usual conscientious manner he will continue to impress. However, not all his work activities will go smoothly and in 1997 he could have some awkward matters to contend with. Fortunately, though, the Earth Dog has a resolute streak in him as well as a sharp mind and while lesser personalities may give up in the face of difficulties, he will rise up and surmount any challenges. In doing so, he will enhance his reputation even further. Indeed, many Earth Dogs will find that out of the several problems they face over the year, new opportunities will emerge and some of the events that occur – worrying though they may be at the time – could come to be viewed as blessings in disguise. The problems that do occur could be of a bureaucratic nature or caused by the obstructionist attitude of others; in either case the Earth Dog's skill, together with his persistent and personable nature, will do much to remedy the situation. Most of the difficulties will arise in the first half of the year and it will be in the latter part of the Ox year and in 1998 that the Earth Dog will see the real rewards of his efforts. Those Earth Dogs wanting to change their position or seeking work should continue to follow up any opportunities that they see but also investigate types of work they have not undertaken before. They could find their persistence will be rewarded in quite an unexpected way and that by taking on a new type of work they will be able to develop fresh talents. This again will help their progress all the more in 1998. As far as financial matters are concerned, the Earth Dog could face some expense concerned with his accommodation and transport over the year and to prevent problems occurring, he does need to make allowances for this in his budget. He would also be helped if he were to check his regular outgoings and cut back on any expenses that may no longer be essential. His domestic life will be busy but generally enjoyable. However, there will be several important family matters that do require his attention and those around him will greatly appreciate his efforts, sound advice and support. Similarly, the Earth Dog should actively involve his family in his own activities and will find much value and comfort in discussing any problems or uncertainties he has with them. He may not always have as much time for socializing or his own interests as he may like this year but he should still ensure that he allows time to spend with his friends and to attend to his various interests. Both can bring him much pleasure as well as provide him with an important source of relaxation. Challenging though the year may be, the Earth Dog will learn and gain much from its events and this will help him to make more substantial progress in 1998. In many respects, what the

Earth Dog achieves in the Ox year will be preparing the way for his future advances.

FAMOUS DOGS

André Agassi, Jane Asher, Brigitte Bardot, Dr Christiaan Barnard, Candice Bergman, Dr Boutros Boutros-Ghali, David Bowie, Kate Bush, Max Bygraves, Naomi Campbell, King Carl Gustaf XVI of Sweden, Belinda Carlisle, José Carreras, Cher, Sir Winston Churchill, Petula Clark, Bill Clinton, Leonard Cohen, Robin Cook, Jacques Cousteau, Jamie Lee Curtis, Charles Dance, Daniel Day Lewis, Christopher Dean, Sally Field, Robert Frost, Judy Garland, George Gershwin, Lenny Henry, Patricia Hodge, Victor Hugo, Barry Humphries, Michael Jackson, Henry Kelly, Felicity Kendal, Sue Lawley, Maureen Lipman, Sophia Loren, Joanna Lumley, Shirley MacLaine, Patrick MacNee, Madonna, Norman Mailer, Winnie Mandela, Barry Manilow, Rik Mayall, Golda Meir, Freddie Mercury, Hayley Mills, Liza Minnelli, David Niven, Elvis Presley, Priscilla Presley, Artist formerly known as Prince, Yitzhak Rabin, Anneka Rice, Wendy Richard, Malcolm Rifkind, George Robertson, Paul Robeson, Linda Ronstadt, Gabriela Sabatini, Sade, Jennifer Saunders, Claudia Schiffer, Norman Schwarzkopf, Dr Albert Schweitzer, Clare Short, Sylvester Stallone, Sharon Stone, Jack Straw, David Suchet, Donald Sutherland, Chris Tarrant, Mother Teresa, Ben Vereen, Timothy West, Mary Whitehouse, Prince William, Shelley Winters.

30 JANUARY 1911 ～ 17 FEBRUARY 1912		*Metal Pig*
16 FEBRUARY 1923 ～ 4 FEBRUARY 1924		*Water Pig*
4 FEBRUARY 1935 ～ 23 JANUARY 1936		*Wood Pig*
22 JANUARY 1947 ～ 9 FEBRUARY 1948		*Fire Pig*
8 FEBRUARY 1959 ～ 27 JANUARY 1960		*Earth Pig*
27 JANUARY 1971 ～ 14 FEBRUARY 1972		*Metal Pig*
13 FEBRUARY 1983 ～ 1 FEBRUARY 1984		*Water Pig*
31 JANUARY 1995 ～ 18 FEBRUARY 1996		*Wood Pig*

T H E
PIG

THE PERSONALITY OF THE PIG

> Life is a series of experiences, each one of which makes us
> bigger, even though sometimes it is hard to realize this.
>
> *– Henry Ford: a Pig*

The Pig is born under the sign of honesty. He has a kind
and understanding nature and is well known for his abilities as a peace-maker. He hates any sort of discord or
unpleasantness and will do all in his power to sort out
differences of opinion or bring opposing factions together.

He is an excellent conversationalist and speaks truth-
fully and to the point. He dislikes any form of falsehood or
hypocrisy and is a firm believer in justice and the maintenance of law and order. In spite of these beliefs, however, the
Pig is reasonably tolerant and often prepared to forgive
others for their wrongs. He rarely harbours grudges and is
never vindictive.

The Pig is usually very popular. He enjoys other people's
company and likes to be involved in joint or group activities. He will be a loyal member of any club or society and
can be relied upon to lend a helping hand at functions. He
is also an excellent fund-raiser for charities and often a
great supporter of humanitarian causes.

The Pig is a hard and conscientious worker and is particularly respected for his reliability and integrity. In his early
years he will try his hand at several different jobs, but he is
usually happiest where he feels that he is being of service to
others. He will unselfishly give up his time for the common
good and is highly valued by his colleagues and employers.

The Pig has a good sense of humour and invariably has a smile, joke or some whimsical remark at the ready. He loves to entertain and to please others, and there are many Pigs who have been attracted to careers in show business or who enjoy following the careers of famous stars and personalities.

There are, unfortunately, some who take advantage of the Pig's good nature and impose on his generosity. The Pig has great difficulty in saying 'No' and, although he may dislike being firm, it would be in his own interests to say occasionally, 'Enough is enough.' The Pig can also be rather naïve and gullible; however, if at any stage in his life he feels that he has been badly let down, he will make sure that it will never happen again and will try to become self-reliant. There are many Pigs who have become entrepreneurs or forged a successful career on their own after some early disappointment in life. And although the Pig tends to spend his money quite freely, he is usually very astute in financial matters and there are many Pigs who have become wealthy.

Another characteristic of the Pig is his ability to recover from set-backs reasonably quickly. His faith and his strength of character keep him going. If he thinks that there is a job he can do or has something that he wants to achieve, he will pursue it with a dogged determination. He can also be stubborn and, no matter how many may plead with him, once he has made his mind up he will rarely change his views.

Although the Pig may work hard, he also knows how to enjoy himself. He is a great pleasure-seeker and will quite happily spend his hard-earned money on a lavish holiday or an expensive meal – for the Pig is a connoisseur of good food and wine – or taking part in a variety of recreational activities. He also enjoys small social gatherings and, if he is in company he likes, can very easily become the life and soul of the party. He does, however, tend to become rather withdrawn at larger functions or when among strangers.

The Pig is also a creature of comfort and his home will usually be fitted with all the latest in luxury appliances. Where possible, he will prefer to live in the country rather than the town and will opt to have a big garden, for the Pig is usually a keen and successful gardener.

The Pig is very popular with the opposite sex and will often have numerous romances before he settles down. Once settled, however, he will be loyal and protective to his partner and he will find that he is especially well-suited to those born under the signs of the Goat, Rabbit, Dog and Tiger, and also to another Pig. Due to his affable and easy-going nature he can also establish a satisfactory relationship with all the remaining signs of the Chinese zodiac, with the exception of the Snake. The Snake tends to be wily, secretive and very guarded, and this can be intensely irritating to the honest and open-hearted Pig.

The female Pig will devote all her energies to the needs of her children and her partner. She will try to ensure that they want for nothing and their pleasure is very much her pleasure. Her home will either be very clean and orderly or hopelessly untidy. Strangely, there seems to be no in between with the Pig – they either love housework or detest it! The female Pig does, however, have considerable talents as an organizer and this, combined with her friendly and open manner, enables her to secure many of her objectives. She can also be a caring and conscientious parent and has very good taste in clothes.

The Pig is usually lucky in life and will rarely want for anything. Provided he does not let others take advantage of his good nature and is not afraid of asserting himself, he will go through life making friends, helping others and winning the admiration of many.

THE FIVE DIFFERENT TYPES OF PIG

In addition to the 12 signs of the Chinese zodiac, there are five elements and these have a strengthening or moderating influence on the sign. The effects of the five elements on the Pig are described below, together with the years in which the elements were exercising their influence. Therefore all Pigs born in 1911 and 1971 are Metal Pigs, those born in 1923 and 1983 are Water Pigs, and so on.

Metal Pig: 1911, 1971

The Metal Pig is more ambitious and determined than some of the other types of Pig. He is strong, energetic and likes to be involved in a wide variety of different activities. He is very open and forthright in his views, although he can be a little too trusting at times and has a tendency to accept things at face value. He has a good sense of humour and loves to attend parties and other social gatherings. He has a warm, outgoing nature and usually has a large circle of friends.

Water Pig: 1923, 1983

The Water Pig has a heart of gold. He is generous and loyal and tries to remain on good terms with everyone. He will do his utmost to help others, but sadly there are some who will take advantage of his kind nature and he should, in his own interests, be a little more discriminating and be prepared to stand firm against anything that he does not like. Although he prefers the quieter things in life, he has a wide range of interests. He particularly enjoys outdoor pursuits and attending parties and social occasions. He is a hard and conscientious worker and invariably does well in his chosen profession. He is also gifted in the art of communication.

Wood Pig: 1935, 1995

This Pig has a friendly, persuasive manner and is easily able to gain the confidence of others. He likes to be involved in all that is going on around him and can some-times take on more responsibility than he can properly handle. He is loyal to his family and friends and he also derives much pleasure from helping those less fortunate than himself. The Wood Pig is usually an optimist and leads a very full, enjoyable and satisfying life. He also has a good sense of humour.

Fire Pig: 1947

The Fire Pig is both energetic and adventurous and he sets about everything he does in a confident and resolute manner. He is very forthright in his views and does not mind taking risks in order to achieve his objectives. He can, however, get carried away by the excitement of the moment and ought to exercise more caution with some of the enterprises in which he gets involved. The Fire Pig is usually lucky in money matters and is well known for his generosity. He is also very caring towards the members of his family.

Earth Pig: 1899, 1959

This Pig has a kindly nature. He is sensible and realistic and will go to great lengths in order to please his employers and to secure his aims and ambitions. He is an excellent organizer and is particularly astute in business and financial matters. He has a good sense of humour and a wide circle of friends. He also likes to lead an active social life, although he does sometimes have a tendency to eat and drink more than is good for him.

PROSPECTS FOR THE PIG IN 1997

The Chinese New Year starts on 7 February 1997. Until then, the old year, the Year of the Rat, is still making its presence felt.

The Year of the Rat (19 February 1996 to 6 February 1997) will have been a generally pleasant year for the Pig and, while he may not always have achieved as much as he would have liked, he will still have made steady progress in many of his activities.

The aspects in the last few months of the year remain

positive and encouraging, and in his work the Pig should continue to set about his duties in his usual diligent manner and remain alert for ways in which he can use his considerable talents. Many Pigs will find themselves being given additional and more interesting responsibilities as the year draws to a close and the Pig will find that any ideas or plans he wishes to develop will generally meet with approval. However, whether in work or seeking work, the Pig should give serious consideration to his future objectives, particularly to what he wishes to attain in 1997. Even more favourable times await him in the next Chinese year and to take advantage of these trends it would benefit him to have some aim or objective to work towards. Anything constructive that he can do at this time – whether in the way of planning or gaining additional experience – would certainly be to his advantage. January 1997 will be a particularly positive month for career matters.

Domestically and socially, the closing months of the Rat year will go well and the Pig can look forward to some pleasing times with those around him. In particular, some social events he attends late in November and early in December will prove most enjoyable and some will give him the chance to meet friends and relations he has not seen for some time. However, with the Pig finding himself so much in demand, he could find he is spending more than anticipated and while his usual shrewd financial sense will enable him to avert problems, he would still do well to watch his level of outgoings. For the unattached Pig, the aspects of the Rat year remain good and there will be further opportunities to make new friends. Also, for the young at heart, romance is very much in the air!

The Pig will also find the latter part of the Rat year a good time to tackle jobs around his home – including some he might have been putting off! – and he will find practical projects will not only go well but be satisfying to carry out. If he has any outstanding tasks, including unanswered correspondence, he should set time aside to attend to these. With a concerted effort early in December he will get a great deal done and this will leave him freer to enjoy the Christmas and New Year holidays as well as start the New Year reasonably up to date.

The Year of the Ox starts on 7 February and generally holds much promise for the Pig. The Ox year very much favours those who are industrious and tenacious, and the Pig is both! However, for the Pig to get the most from this favourable year he does need to work hard and remain committed to his objectives. If he can do this, then he will make excellent progress.

Over the last 12 months the Pig will have greatly impressed others and in the Ox year he will be able to reap the rewards of his past efforts. Many Pigs will be promoted or be successful in obtaining a new and more challenging position. In particular, the Pig should remain alert for opportunities in the first few months of the year and in March 1997 he could discover, quite by chance, an excellent opening to follow. He should also promote any ideas that he has or set in motion any plans he may have been formulating. This is very much a progressive year and by acting positively he can, and will, do well.

In his work the Pig may find himself having to deal with new procedures and techniques, and while he may some-times have misgivings about these, he should not be too resistant to the changes introduced. By being adaptable he will win the support of others – especially those with influence – and this again will help his prospects. One word of warning, though: the Pig does possess a stubborn streak and as far as work matters are concerned, he should not let his stubbornness mar his prospects or undermine the goodwill he has built up.

Many of those Pigs seeking work will find their persistence rewarded quite early in 1997 and they should actively follow up any opportunities they see. They would also do well to get in contact with those who may be in a position to help them or are in a line of work they wish to enter. By doing this they may learn of new possibilities they have not considered before or be given advice that they will find most helpful. By using his initiative the Pig can achieve much and with this being a year for progress, he should make the most of the positive trends that prevail.

The Pig will also fare well in financial matters although if he is able to set any money aside for a specific purpose rather than succumb to too many indulgences, he will be pleased he has done so. In particular, he could consider setting a regular amount to one side for a holiday he would like later in the year or for some items or alterations he would like for his accommodation. He could also enjoy some success with an investment he makes or savings policy he takes out and his shrewd business and financial sense will be as keen as ever. If he is able to set any spare money aside for his longer term future, this too could be to his advantage.

The Pig's domestic life will be busy – sometimes even hectic! – but will contain many satisfying and pleasurable moments. There will also be good reason for him to be involved in a personal celebration. This could be a marriage, an addition to his family or some success he enjoys. Also, those close to the Pig will be most supportive and he will obtain much useful encouragement and help from them. However, at busy times or when he feels under pressure, he should not hesitate to ask for assistance rather than drive on relentlessly. Similarly, should there be any matters concerning him, the Pig should let them be known rather than keep them to himself. To let any worries or doubts linger in his mind could take the edge off what will otherwise be a pleasurable year and sometimes he could even find his worries misplaced.

The Pig's social life will also go well and there will be many opportunities for him to attend social occasions and meet others. Many Pigs will strike up new and important friendships over the year and socially, the Pig will find himself much in demand. Pigs seeking friends or romance will certainly not be disappointed, although they should be wary of building up high expectations after just a brief meeting. Ideally, the Pig should let any new friendship develop in its own time rather than rush into an early commitment; this way the friendship is more likely to be built upon a secure foundation. The months from April to September will be a most propitious time for the Pig's social life, although if he has a heavy workload or is studying for exams, he should not let his social life encroach too much upon what he needs to carry out. The Pig has a great fondness for socializing but in the Ox year he does need to keep things in perspective – 'Work before play' should be his motto!

The Pig will also derive much satisfaction from his interests over the year, especially those that take him out of doors. For the many Pigs who enjoy gardening, this will be a most productive year; similarly, those Pigs who enjoy travel will take much delight in the journeys they go on and places they visits over the year.

With so much going on in the Pig's life in 1997 he should not, however, neglect his own well-being. If he does not get much exercise during the day he should consider undertaking some extra walking or engaging in cycling, swimming or some other suitable activity that will help keep him fit. Similarly, if he relies a lot on convenience foods, he could find switching to a more balanced diet to his advantage. Anything positive that the Pig can do to maintain and improve his well-being will be very much in his interests.

Overall, the Ox year will be a satisfying and enjoyable year for the Pig. However, to take advantage of the positive trends that prevail, he needs to work hard and stay committed to his objectives. The Pig can achieve much in 1997, as well as have a good time, but to achieve the results he wants and is capable of obtaining he does need to give of his best. The Pig has many wonderful and diverse talents; in the Ox year he should make the most of them.

As far as the different types of Pig are concerned, this will be a successful year for the *Metal Pig*. It will not only contain some personally pleasing times for him but there will also be some splendid opportunities which will enable him to improve upon his present position. In recent years the Metal Pig will have gained much valuable experience and this, together with his plans and aspirations, will help him to make further advances. In 1997 he should actively pursue any opportunities he sees and while in some cases these could involve him in a significant change (even a move), anything positive that he can do to further his career would be to his advantage, both now and in the long term. He will also feel stimulated by the changes and challenges that the year brings and will greatly impress those around him with his confident and enterprising manner. Over the year many Metal Pigs will obtain promotion, take on new duties or change to a different type of work. Metal Pigs seeking work should also remain active in their quest and many will find their endeavours rewarded in quite an unexpected way. The Metal Pig will also enjoy good fortune in financial matters, although many Metal Pigs could face some large expenses over the year; this particularly applies to those who change their accommodation. At expensive times and when entering into large transactions, the Metal Pig should make sure he studies the small print carefully and is aware of any obligations he might be placed under. Although he should not experience financial problems in 1997 this is still not a year in which he can afford to be complacent or take undue risks in his financial undertakings. Personally, however, the Ox year will be a time of much happiness. The Metal Pig will take genuine pleasure in the successes enjoyed by those around him and any encouragement or advice he feels able to give to family or close friends will be much appreciated. He will also obtain valuable support for his own activities and at all times would do well to listen carefully to the advice he is given. Those around him speak with his best interests at heart and there will be much wisdom in what he is told. Also, on a personal level, there will be more than one event in 1997 which will give cause for rejoicing. This can include the fulfilment of a long-held ambition. The summer, in particular, will be a most gratifying time. The Metal Pig's social life will also go well and while he may not always have as much time to spend socializing as he has done in the past, he can still look forward to some pleasing times with his many friends. For the Metal Pig who moves to a new area or changes jobs, there will certainly be opportunities to establish a new social life and make new friends. In almost all areas of his life, the aspects are positive and by setting about his activities in his usual determined manner, the Metal Pig can do well. This is a year for action and advance, and the rewards for the determined Metal Pig can be quite substantial.

This will be both a pleasant and constructive year for the *Water Pig*. He will be able to make good progress with many of his activities and will find that the events of the year will generally move in his favour. For those Water Pigs involved in education this will prove both an important and successful year. The time they devote to their studies will be well rewarded and a new subject that they start could prove very significant to their future. Admittedly, they might find some of the work asked of them initially daunting, but they will find their perseverance will be amply rewarded and that in case of difficulty, they should not hesitate to seek assistance. Those around the Water Pig are keen to help and see him make the most of his abilities and throughout the year he should remember that if there is any matter concerning him, he should seek advice rather than keep the worry to himself. This also applies to those Water Pigs born in 1923 – those around them are more than happy to give assistance should they require it and they could find their concerns easily rectified or even unfounded. The Water Pig's domestic and social life will be active as well as give him much satisfaction. There will also be opportunities for him to make some new friends over the year and any Water Pig who may have had to contend with some recent sadness or is feeling lonely should make every effort to go out more and get in contact with others. In particular, a holiday that he takes will lead to some new friendships and if he is able to join a local club or society, this too will lead to some pleasurable occasions. The Water Pig will also delight in the success enjoyed by a near relation and many Water Pigs will find themselves actively participating in a major family celebration over the year! The Water Pig will also obtain much satisfaction from his hobbies and for those creatively inclined, it could be in their interests to enter a suitable competition or bring their work to the notice of others. By doing so they could find their efforts highly praised and well rewarded. The Water Pig will fare well in financial matters in 1997 and by remaining alert could obtain some items for himself and his home at most favourable prices. However, while much of 1997 is well aspected, there are two areas in which he does need to exercise caution. The first concerns matters of a bureau-cratic nature. If he receives any important forms or corre-spondence, he needs to deal with these with care and should he have any doubts over what is being asked, he should check rather than guess. If not properly handled, matters involving paperwork could take some time to sort out. Care is also needed if the Water Pig has to move heavy items or use potentially dangerous appliances. This is not a year when he can take risks with his personal safely and in any strenuous or hazardous undertaking he needs to take all the precautions necessary. These warnings apart, this will be a most satisfying year for the Water Pig and by using his time wisely, he will be well pleased with what he achieves and the happiness that the year will bring.

This will be an important year for the *Wood Pig* and one which will see several significant changes. While these changes will give times of uncertainty and pressure, events will work out in the Wood Pig's favour. In particular, accommodation matters will figure prominently over the year. Some Wood Pigs will move while others will redecorate or carry out extensive improvements; in either case this will take up a considerable amount of the Wood Pig's time, but he will be well satisfied with the end result. Wood Pigs who move will feel stimulated by the change that living in a new area will bring and will delight in discovering the amenities and opportunities on offer. With their amiable nature, they are also likely to establish a new social life quite quickly and will make some meaningful friendships as the year progresses. For the Wood Pig in work, this will be a year of change and decision-making. Some Wood Pigs will be offered new and more varied responsibilities and will rise up to the challenges placed before them, while others will consider retiring or moving to less strenuous duties. In either case, the Wood Pig will be pleased with his decisions and actions, but in arriving at these decisions he should take his time and not take any irrevocable action until he is satisfied it is the right course to take. He will find his family and friends most helpful and encouraging when he does need to take important decisions. He will also enjoy good fortune in financial matters and many Wood Pigs will receive an additional sum of money for some work they have carried out in the past or from an unexpected source. Also, with luck on his side, it could also be worth the Wood Pig entering any competition that catches his eye over the year. However, while he will certainly enjoy this upturn in his finances, it would still be in his interests to consider setting some money aside for his future; he could be grateful for this in later years. Both domestically and socially the year will go well for the Wood Pig and he can look forward to some pleasing times with his family and friends. He will find joint activities especially gratifying and would do well to encourage pursuits that others can join in with. This includes household projects, various hobbies and interests and trips out. The Wood Pig will also enjoy the travelling that he undertakes over the year and a holiday or break he takes in the late summer could turn out to be one of the best he has had for a long time. Generally, 1997 will be a pleasant and constructive year for the Wood Pig and by setting about his activities in an organized and efficient manner he can accomplish much.

Over the last few years the *Fire Pig* will have given much thought to some projects and plans that he would like to carry out. In the Ox year he will be given a chance to put some of these into practice. For the bold and enterprising Fire Pig – and there are many – this will be a year of considerable opportunity. Throughout, the Fire Pig should seize any chance that he has to promote himself, his work or his ideas. Those around him will look favourably on his undertakings as well as admire his resolve and determination. In 1997 the Fire Pig can make progress in almost any area of his life and providing he remains committed to his objectives, he will do well. In his work he should keep alert for opportunities to pursue and investigate ways in which he can put his considerable talents to best use. He could find discussions with those who are in a position to advise him particularly beneficial and he should not hesitate to put forward any ideas and suggestions he might have. He will be at his most impressive during the Ox year and should capitalize on the favourable trends that prevail. Many Fire Pigs will find their efforts rewarded with greater responsibilities or be successful in gaining the type of work they have been wanting for some time. The early months of the year are especially favourable for career matters and all Fire Pigs, whether in work or seeking work, should remain alert for openings at this time. The Fire Pig will also enjoy an improvement in his financial situation over the year and while he will delight in buying some items for himself, his loved ones and his home, it would be in his interests to save any surplus money he might have for his longer term future. An investment made in 1997 could work out most successfully for him and build into a useful asset in years to come. The Fire Pig's domestic and social life will also go well and he can look forward to some pleasurable times with those around him. Many Fire Pigs will also be involved in a family celebration over the year, possibly through the marriage of a close relation or birth of a grandchild, and some family events that take place will be a source of considerable pride to him. He will also be pleased with some work that he carries out on his accommodation and garden over the year and generally projects of a practical nature will give him much satisfaction. Most of what the Fire Pig undertakes in 1997 will go well and those around him will be both encouraging and supportive. In the Ox year he can accomplish much, but to make the most of this favourable year he needs to decide upon his objectives and then set about them in his usual illustrious way.

In recent years the *Earth Pig* will have gained much valuable experience as well as impressed those around him. In 1997 his past efforts will be rewarded. The Ox year is one for positive advance and the Earth Pig can look forward to success in many of his ventures. In his work he will enjoy some pleasing developments as well as some splendid strokes of good fortune. Some Earth Pigs will be offered promotion or increased responsibilities – sometimes quite unexpectedly – while others will be given opportunities to develop some ideas and plans they have been contemplating. Those around the Earth Pig will be most supportive and Earth Pigs who are ambitious to get on should actively pursue any opportunities or openings that they see. With determination and resolve, great progress will be possible. Similarly, many of the Earth Pigs seeking work will find their persistence rewarded, sometimes in quite an unexpected and fortuitous way. These Earth Pigs would also be helped if they were to make direct contact with those in a position to advise or assist them; anything constructive they can do will repay them handsomely. The Earth Pig should also keep himself well-informed about all that is going on around him. This way he could learn of some information or opportunities that could turn out useful for him. The Earth Pig can also look forward to an improvement in his financial situation over the year and this will enable many Earth Pigs to complete some work or improvements on their accommodation they have been considering for some time. Domestically and socially, this will also be a pleasing year and the Earth Pig will have some most enjoyable times with those around him. The progress of a younger relation in particular will be a great source of pride to him and any additional support and encouragement he feels able to give will be much valued. Although the Earth Pig may feel that he does not have as much time to devote to his hobbies as he may like, these do provide him with an important source of relaxation and it would be very much in his interests to set a regular time aside for recreational pursuits. Over the year his interests, especially those of a creative nature, could provide him with much pleasure as well as prove most beneficial for him. Overall, 1997 will be a positive year for the Earth Pig and it would be in his interests to promote himself and his ideas as much as he can. Positive action on his part will lead to considerable progress and benefit.

FAMOUS PIGS

Russ Abbot, Bryan Adams, Woody Allen, Julie Andrews, Fred Astaire, Sir Richard Attenborough, Lucielle Ball, Hector Berlioz, David Blunkett, Humphrey Bogart, James Cagney, Maria Callas, Dr George Carey, Richard Chamberlain, Jack Charlton, Hillary Rodham Clinton, Glenn Close, Andy Cole, David Coultard, Sir Noël Coward, Oliver Cromwell, Billy Crystal, the Dalai Lama, Bobby Davro, Phil Donahue, Richard Dreyfuss, Sheena Easton, Ben Elton, Ralph Waldo Emerson, David Essex, Farrah Fawcett, Henry Ford, Emmylou Harris, Chesney Hawkes, William Randolph Hearst, Ernest Hemingway, Henry VIII, Alfred Hitchcock, King Hussein of Jordan, Elton John, C. G. Jung, Stephen King, Nastassja Kinski, Henry Kissinger, Kevin Kline, Hugh Laurie, Jerry Lee Lewis, John McEnroe, Marcel Marceau, Johnny Mathis, Dudley Moore, Patrick Moore, Morrissey, John Mortimer, Wolfgang Amadeus Mozart, Marie Osmond, Michael Parkinson, Luciano Pavarotti, Shimon Peres, Lester Piggott, Prince Rainier of Monaco, Charlotte Rampling, Maurice Ravel, Dan Quayle, Ronald Reagan, Lee Remick, Ginger Rogers, Nick Ross, Salman Rushdie, Baroness Sue Ryder of Warsaw, Pete Sampras, Arantxa Sanchez, Carlos Santana, Arnold Schwarzenegger, Donald Sinden, Steven Spielberg, Emma Thompson, Topol, Tracey Ullman, Michael Winner, the Duchess of York.

APPENDIX

———◆———

The relationship between the 12 animal signs – both on a personal level and business level – is an important aspect of Chinese horoscopes and in this appendix the compatibility between the signs is shown in the two tables that follow. Also included are the names of the signs ruling the hours of the day and from this it is possible to find your ascendant and discover yet another aspect of your personality.

PERSONAL RELATIONSHIPS

KEY
1 Excellent. Great rapport.
2 A successful relationship. Many interests in common.
3 Mutual respect and understanding. A good relationship.
4 Fair. Needs care and some willingness to compromise in order for the relationship to work.
5 Awkward. Possible difficulties in communication with few interests in common.
6 A clash of personalities. Very difficult.

	Rat	Ox	Tiger	Rabbit	Dragon	Snake	Horse	Goat	Monkey	Rooster	Dog	Pig
Rat	1											
Ox	1	3										
Tiger	4	6	5									
Rabbit	5	2	3	2								
Dragon	1	5	4	3	2							
Snake	3	1	6	2	1	5						
Horse	6	5	1	5	3	4	2					
Goat	5	5	3	1	4	3	2	2				
Monkey	1	3	6	3	1	3	5	3	1			
Rooster	5	1	5	6	2	1	2	5	5	5		
Dog	3	4	1	2	6	3	1	5	3	5	2	
Pig	2	3	2	2	2	6	3	2	2	3	1	2

BUSINESS RELATIONSHIPS

KEY
1 Excellent. Marvellous understanding and rapport.
2 Very good. Complement each other well.
3 A good working relationship and understanding can be developed.
4 Fair, but compromise and a common objective is often needed to make this relationship work.
5 Awkward. Unlikely to work, either through lack of trust, understanding or the competitiveness of the signs.
6 Mistrust. Difficult. To be avoided.

	Rat	Ox	Tiger	Rabbit	Dragon	Snake	Horse	Goat	Monkey	Rooster	Dog	Pig
Rat	2											
Ox	1	3										
Tiger	3	6	5									
Rabbit	4	3	3	3								
Dragon	1	4	3	3	3							
Snake	3	2	6	4	1	5						
Horse	6	5	1	5	3	4	4					
Goat	5	5	3	1	4	3	3	2				
Monkey	2	3	4	5	1	5	4	4	3			
Rooster	5	1	5	5	2	1	2	5	5	6		
Dog	4	5	2	3	6	4	2	5	3	5	4	
Pig	3	3	3	2	3	5	4	2	3	4	3	1

YOUR ASCENDANT

The ascendant has a very strong influence on your personality and, together with the information already given about your sign and the effects of the element on your sign, it will help you gain even greater insight into your true personality according to Chinese horoscopes.

The hours of the day are named after the 12 animal signs and the sign governing the time you were born is your ascendant. To find your ascendant, look up the time of your birth on the table below, bearing in mind any local time differences in the place you were born.

11 p.m.	to	1 a.m.	The hours of the Rat
1 a.m.	to	3 a.m.	The hours of the Ox
3 a.m.	to	5 a.m.	The hours of the Tiger
5 a.m.	to	7 a.m.	The hours of the Rabbit
7 a.m.	to	9 a.m.	The hours of the Dragon
9 a.m.	to	11 a.m.	The hours of the Snake
11 a.m.	to	1 p.m.	The hours of the Horse
1 p.m.	to	3 p.m.	The hours of the Goat
3 p.m.	to	5 p.m.	The hours of the Monkey
5 p.m.	to	7 p.m.	The hours of the Rooster
7 p.m.	to	9 p.m.	The hours of the Dog
9 p.m.	to	11 p.m.	The hours of the Pig

RAT: The influence of the Rat as ascendant is likely to make the sign more outgoing, more sociable and also more careful with money. A particularly beneficial influence for those born under the sign of the Rabbit, Horse, Monkey and Pig.

OX: The Ox as ascendant has a restraining, cautionary and steadying influence which many signs will benefit from. This ascendant also promotes self-confidence and will-power and is an especially good ascendant for those born under the signs of the Tiger, Rabbit and Goat.

TIGER: This ascendant is a dynamic and stirring influence which makes the sign more outgoing, more action-orientated and more impulsive. A generally favourable ascendant for the Ox, Tiger, Snake and Horse.

RABBIT: The Rabbit as ascendant has a moderating influence, making the sign more reflective, serene and discreet. A particularly beneficial influence for the Rat, Dragon, Monkey and Rooster.

DRAGON: The Dragon as ascendant gives strength, determination and an added ambition to the sign. A favourable influence for those born under the signs of the Rabbit, Goat, Monkey and Dog.

SNAKE: The Snake as ascendant can make the sign more reflective, more intuitive and more self-reliant. A good influence for the Tiger, Goat and Pig.

HORSE: The influence of the Horse will make the sign more adventurous, more daring and, on some occasions, more fickle. Generally a beneficial influence for the Rabbit, Snake, Dog and Pig.

GOAT: This ascendant will make the sign more tolerant,

easy-going and receptive. The Goat could also impart some creative and artistic qualities to the sign. An especially good influence for the Ox, Dragon, Snake and Rooster.

MONKEY: The Monkey as ascendant is likely to impart a delicious sense of humour and fun to the sign. He will make the sign more enterprising and outgoing – a particularly good influence for the Rat, Ox, Snake and Goat.

ROOSTER: The Rooster as ascendant helps to give the sign a lively, outgoing and very methodical manner. Its influence will increase efficiency and is good for the Ox, Tiger, Rabbit and Horse.

DOG: The Dog as ascendant makes the sign more reasonable and fair-minded as well as giving an added sense of loyalty. A very good ascendant for the Tiger, Dragon and Goat.

PIG: The influence of the Pig can make the sign more sociable, content and self-indulgent. It is also a caring influence and one which can make the sign want to help others. A good ascendant for the Dragon and Monkey.

HOW TO GET THE BEST
FROM YOUR CHINESE SIGN
AND THE YEAR

To supplement the earlier chapters on the personality and horoscope of the signs, I have included in this appendix a guide on how you can get the best out of your sign and the year.

Each of the 12 Chinese signs possesses its own unique strengths and by identifying them you can use them to your advantage. Similarly, by becoming aware of possible weaknesses you can do much to rectify them and in this respect I hope the following sections will be useful. Also included are some tips on how you can get the best from this most interesting of Chinese years. The areas covered are general prospects, career prospects, finance and relations with others.

THE RAT

The Rat is blessed with many fine talents but his undoubted strength lies in his ability to get on with others. He is sociable, charming and a good judge of character. He also possesses a shrewd mind and is good at spotting opportunities.

However, to make the most of himself and his abilities, the Rat does need to impose some discipline upon himself. He should resist the temptation (sometimes very great!) of getting involved in too many activities all at the same time and decide upon his priorities and objectives. By concentrating his energies on specific matters he will fare much better as a result. Also, given his personable manner, he should seek out positions where he can use his personal relations skills to good effect. For a career, sales and marketing could prove ideal.

The Rat is also astute in dealing with finance but, while often thrifty, he can sometimes give way to moments of indulgence. Although he deserves to enjoy the money he has so carefully earned, it may sometimes be in his interests to exercise more restraint when tempted to satisfy too many extravagant whims!

The Rat's family and friends are also most important to him and while he is loyal and protective towards them, he does tend to keep his worries and concerns to himself. He would be helped if he were more willing to discuss any anxieties he has. Those around the Rat think highly of him and are prepared to do much to help him, but for them to do this he does need to be less secretive and guarded.

With his sharp mind, keen imagination and sociable manner, the Rat does, however, have much in his favour. First, though, he should decide what he wants to achieve and then concentrate upon his chosen objectives. When he has commitment, the Rat can be irrepressible and, given his considerable charm, he can often be irresistible as well! Provided he channels his energies wisely he can make much of his life.

Advice for the Rat's Year Ahead

GENERAL PROSPECTS

A relatively good year for the Rat and provided he is prepared to work hard and remains committed to his objectives, he can achieve much.

CAREER PROSPECTS

This is a year which holds considerable potential for the Rat. However, to make the most of it, he cannot afford to rest on his laurels, take risks or depend solely upon his charm and persuasive talents to get results. This is a year for hard work. For those Rats who are prepared to make the effort, the rewards can be substantial. The Rat would do well to concentrate on areas in which he is most experienced and avoid committing himself to major new projects without a thorough investigation. The determined and committed Rat can make considerable progress over the year.

FINANCE

Although not a bad year for financial matters, caution is needed. The Rat would do well to plan major purchases rather than give way to impulse buying and also to avoid risky undertakings. He is usually careful and thrifty when dealing with finance and in the Ox year he should try not to let his generally disciplined manner slip.

RELATIONS WITH OTHERS

The Rat's social and domestic life will be busy in 1997 but bring him much pleasure. For those seeking romance and new friends, this will also be a good year. However, the Rat can at times be pernickety and demanding, and he would do well to watch this with family members. To expect his own way all the time could cause friction and take the edge off what will be an otherwise pleasant year.

THE OX

Strong-willed, determined and resolute, the Ox certainly has a mind of his own! He is also persistent and sets about achieving his objectives with a dogged determination. In addition, he is reliable and tenacious and is often a source of inspiration to others. The Ox is a doer and an achiever and in life he often accomplishes much. However, for him to really excel, he would do well to try and correct his weaknesses.

Being so resolute and having such a strong sense of purpose, the Ox can be inflexible and narrow-minded. He can be resistant to change and prefers to set about his activities in his own way rather than be too dependent on others. He should aim to be more outgoing and adventurous in his outlook. His dislike of change can sometimes be to his detriment and if he were prepared to be more adaptable he could find his progress both easier and smoother.

The Ox would also be helped if he were to broaden his range of interests and become more relaxed in his approach. At times he can be so preoccupied with his own activities that he is not always as mindful of others as he should be and his demeanour can sometimes be studious and serious. There are times when he would benefit from a lighter touch.

However, the Ox is true to his word and loyal to his family and friends. He is admired and respected by others and his tremendous will-power usually enables him to secure much in life.

Advice for the Ox's Year Ahead

GENERAL PROSPECTS
A pleasant and productive year for the Ox.

CAREER PROSPECTS
In 1997 the Ox will be given every opportunity to further his plans and ideas as well as to consolidate his position. He will make steady progress and will impress and gain support from those around him. This is also an excellent year for him to add to his skills and all Oxen would do well to try and go on training courses or undertake some additional study. Anything positive the Ox can do will repay him handsomely both in this and future years.

FINANCE
The Ox will enjoy an improvement in his financial position although he could still face several large expenses over the year. With his usual good care and sensible budgeting, these should not cause him too many problems. However, the Ox should be wary of risky or speculative ventures and if he has any doubts he should seek further advice.

RELATIONS WITH OTHERS

This will be a year of much personal happiness. For the unattached Ox there will be the chance of new and meaningful friendships, romance and marriage, while other Oxen will take much delight in their domestic and social lives. This is the Ox's own year and will be, as far as his relations with others are concerned, one he will very much enjoy. However, being as strong-minded as he is, the Ox should not allow any minor disagreement that may occur to escalate and spoil an otherwise excellent year. Oxen, be warned – and enjoy your year!

THE TIGER

Lively, innovative and enterprising, the Tiger is one who enjoys an active lifestyle. He has a wide range of interests, an alert mind and a genuine liking of others. He likes to live life to the full. However, despite his enthusiastic and well-meaning ways, he does not always make the most of his considerable potential.

By being so versatile, the Tiger does have a tendency to jump from one activity to another or dissipate his energies by trying to do too much at any one time. To make the most of himself he should try to exercise a certain amount of self-discipline. Ideally, he should decide how best he can use his abilities, give himself some objectives and stick with these. If he can overcome his restless tendencies and persist in what he does, he will find he will accomplish much more.

Also, in spite of his sociable manner, the Tiger likes to

retain a certain independence in his actions and while few begrudge him this, he would sometimes find life easier if he were more prepared to work in conjunction with others. His reliance upon his own judgement does sometimes mean that he excludes the views and advice of those around him, and this can be to his detriment. The Tiger may possess an independent spirit but he must not let his independence go too far!

The Tiger does, however, have much in his favour. He is bold, original and quick-witted. If he can keep his restless nature in check he can enjoy considerable success. In addition, his engaging personality makes him one who is much admired and well-liked.

Advice for the Tiger's Year Ahead

GENERAL PROSPECTS
Although the Tiger may not achieve all that he would like over the year, he will nevertheless gain much valuable experience and help to lay the foundations for the better times that await him in 1998.

CAREER PROSPECTS
The Tiger needs to set about his duties carefully and cautiously and at all times remain mindful of the views of his colleagues. This is not a year in which he can afford to be too independent in his actions, take undue risks or start major new projects.

However, by persisting in his duties and giving of his best, he will impress others and this will lead to further progress in the near future. Tigers seeking work should persist in following up any opportunities they see – their efforts could be rewarded in quite a surprising way.

FINANCE

Again, care is needed. This is not a year for speculating or for taking risks. The Tiger should plan his major purchases carefully and when reasonably large sums of money are involved, avoid impulse buying. Generally, it would be in his interests to watch his level of spending throughout the year.

RELATIONS WITH OTHERS

The Tiger can look forward to some enjoyable times with those around him and although his domestic life will be busy, it will bring him much satisfaction. However, he does need to remain mindful of the views of those around him and in awkward moments remain tactful and diplomatic. Those close to him hold him in high esteem and he should not jeopardize the normally good relations he enjoys with them by either being too independent-minded or unduly stubborn.

THE RABBIT

The Rabbit is certainly one who appreciates the finer things in life. With his good taste, companionable nature and wide range of interests, he knows how to live well – and usually does!

However, for all his finesse and style, the Rabbit does possess traits he would do well to watch. His desire for a settled lifestyle makes him err on the side of caution. He dislikes change and as a consequence can miss out on opportunities. Also, there are many Rabbits who will go great lengths to avoid difficult and fraught situations, and again, while few may relish these, sometimes in life it is necessary to take risks or stand your ground just to get on. At times it would certainly be in the Rabbit's interests to be bolder and more assertive in going after whatever he desires.

The Rabbit also attaches great importance to his relations with others and while he has a happy knack of getting on with most, he can be sensitive to criticism. In this, difficult though it may be, he should really try to develop a thicker skin. He should recognize that criticism, as well as some of the problems that occur in life (and which he strives so much to avoid), can be constructive and provide valuable learning opportunities.

The Rabbit, though, with his agreeable manner, keen intellect and shrewd judgement, does have much in his favour and invariably makes much of his life – and usually enjoys it too!

Advice for the Rabbit's Year Ahead

GENERAL PROSPECTS

A variable year. Progress will be slow and the Rabbit will have to reappraise some of his plans. However, out of this, he will emerge wiser, more experienced and with a clearer idea of his future aspirations. This may not be an easy year but its long-term significance cannot be underestimated.

CAREER PROSPECTS

A year of modest progress. Throughout 1997 the Rabbit should stick to areas in which he has most experience rather than take risks or start ambitious new projects. He should also stay alert to all that is happening around him and remain mindful of the views of his colleagues. With care and his usual good sense he will greatly impress others and sow the seeds for future advancement. He would also do well to give consideration to his longer term plans.

FINANCE

The Rabbit will be particularly pleased with some purchases he makes for his accommodation over the year, especially those that relate to decor. However, he would do well to keep a close watch over his general level of spending and avoid risky undertakings. Generally, this is a year for care and restraint.

RELATIONS WITH OTHERS

While the Ox year will contain some testing moments for the Rabbit, his family and friends will be a source of considerable pleasure. They will offer encouragement, support and advice as well as providing the Rabbit with some meaningful and enjoyable times. Personal relations are of great value to the Rabbit and this will be emphasized throughout the year. Rabbits seeking new friends or romance should make every effort to go out more and get in contact with others – it will be well worth their effort.

THE DRAGON

Enthusiastic, enterprising and honourable, the Dragon possesses many admirable qualities and his life is often full and varied. He is always one who gives of his best and even though not all his endeavours may meet with success, he is nonetheless resilient and hardy. As a person, he is much admired and respected.

However, for all his many qualities, the Dragon can be blunt and forthright and, through sheer strength of character, sometimes domineering. It would certainly be in his interests to listen more closely to others rather than be so self-reliant. Also his enthusiasm can sometimes get the better of him and he can be impulsive. To make the most of his abilities, he should set himself priorities and set about his activities in a disciplined and systematic way. More tact and diplomacy might not come amiss either!

However, with his lively and outgoing manner, the Dragon is popular and well-liked. With good fortune on his side (and the Dragon is often lucky), his life is almost certain to be eventful and fulfilling. He has many talents and if he uses them wisely he will enjoy much success.

Advice for the Dragon's Year Ahead

GENERAL PROSPECTS
A pleasant and generally constructive year, although the Dragon should avoid taking unnecessary risks or pushing his Dragon luck too far!

CAREER PROSPECTS

A year of reasonable progress. Although the Dragon may hold very definite ideas on what he wants to do and achieve, in 1997 he must be prepared to accept and adapt to the conditions that prevail. This is just not a year when he can afford to be too independent in his actions and in all that he does he must work closely with others. With care he can make progress and improve upon his position but his chief gains will come from the experience and skills he is able to acquire over the year. These will prove of considerable value in the future.

FINANCE

In 1997 the Dragon must watch his outgoings carefully. This is not a year for entering risky or speculative undertakings or for spending without due regard to his financial situation. Care, caution and prudence are essential if he is to avoid problems later.

RELATIONS WITH OTHERS

The Dragon delights in the company of others and his personal life will provide him with much pleasure over the year. His family and social life will both go well and those around him will be supportive and encouraging. However, in 1997, the Dragon does need to be mindful of others and in any awkward situation exercise tact and discretion. To be unduly stubborn or forthright could undermine the good relations he so much enjoys. However, there will be many opportunities for him to add to his circle of friends and, for the unattached, romance is well aspected.

THE SNAKE

The Snake is blessed with a keen intellect. He has wide interests, an enquiring mind and good judgement. He tends to be quiet and thoughtful and plans his activities with considerable care. With his fine abilities he often does well in life, but he does possess traits which can undermine his progress.

The Snake is often guarded in his actions and sometimes loses out to those who are more action-oriented and assertive. He can also be a loner and likes to retain a certain independence in his actions, and this too can hamper his progress. It would be in his interests to be more forthcoming and involve others more readily in his plans. The Snake has many talents and possesses a warm and rich personality but there is a danger that this can remain concealed behind his often quiet and reserved manner. It really would be in his interests to aim to be more outgoing and show others his true worth.

However, the Snake is very much his own master. He invariably knows what he wants in life and is often prepared to journey long and hard to achieve his objectives. He does, though, have it in his power to make that journey easier. Lose some of that reticence, Snake, be more open, be more assertive and do not be afraid of the occasional risk!

Advice for the Snake's Year Ahead

GENERAL PROSPECTS
A reasonable year but the Snake does need to exercise care with his various activities. This is not a year when he can afford to be too independent in his actions.

CAREER PROSPECTS

Progress is possible but the Snake will need to work hard and apply himself. He should stick to areas in which he has most experience as well as actively promote his ideas. With effort, careful planning and the support of others, he can make pleasing headway. But for those Snakes who are prepared to sit back or rest content with their current situation, progress will be limited and there could be disappointments in store. The Snake would do well to remember that the Ox year particularly rewards those who are prepared to give of their best.

FINANCE

The Snake will need to remain his vigilant self when dealing with financial matters. This is not a year for taking risks or complacency and it would be in his interests to watch his outgoings with care. He should also avoid succumbing to too many extravagant whims.

RELATIONS WITH OTHERS

The Snake's family and social life will bring him much pleasure, but it is important he listens closely to others and remains mindful of their views and advice. The Snake may like to retain a certain independence in his actions, but to get the best results he does need to act in conjunction with those around him. Snakes seeking new friends or romance will enjoy the year.

THE HORSE

Versatile, hard-working and sociable, the Horse makes his mark wherever he goes. He has an eloquent and engaging manner and makes friends with ease. He is quick-witted, has an alert mind and is certainly not averse to taking risks or experimenting with new ideas.

The Horse possesses a strong and likeable personality but he does also have his weaknesses. With his wide interests he does not always finish everything he starts and he would do well to be more persevering. He has it within him to achieve considerable success but when he has made his plans he should stick with them. To make the most of his talents he does need to overcome his restless tendencies.

The Horse loves company and values both his family and friends. However, there will have been many a time when he has spoken in haste and regretted his words or lost his temper. Throughout his life, the Horse needs to keep his temper in check and learn to be diplomatic in tense situations. If not, he could risk jeopardizing the respect and good relations he so much values by a thoughtless remark or action.

The Horse though, has a multitude of talents and a lively and outgoing personality. If he can overcome his restless and volatile nature, he can lead a rich and highly fulfilling life.

Advice for the Horse's Year Ahead

GENERAL PROSPECTS
A year for the Horse to put past problems and uncertainties behind him and look forward to an upturn in his

fortunes that will be with him for several years! This will be a constructive and positive year.

CAREER PROSPECTS

The Horse has a fine reputation for being a hard and determined worker and this will serve him well in the Ox year. His skills and experience will be in demand and he should aim to make the most of himself. He should pursue the opportunities that he sees as well as look for ways in which he can use his considerable talents. With determination, enterprise and persistence he can make substantial progress. A good year for career matters.

FINANCE

The Horse can look forward to an upturn in his financial situation. However, he should make sure he puts his money to good use rather than succumb to too many extravagances or expensive whims! He could, however, be successful in an investment he makes or a savings policy he starts and will also take much delight in improving his accommodation. With care, the Horse can do well in money matters.

RELATIONS WITH OTHERS

Considerable care is needed. Throughout the Ox year the Horse must listen closely to others and act with consideration and forethought. This is just not a year in which he can be too independent in his actions or become so preoccupied with his own activities that he neglects the interests of those around him. In 1997 he must remain mindful of others. Providing he heeds this advice, then both his domestic and social life can bring him much happiness.

THE GOAT

The Goat has a warm, friendly and understanding manner and gets on well with most. He is generally easy-going, has a fond appreciation of the finer things in life and possesses a rich imagination. He is often artistic, enjoys the creative arts and outdoor activities.

However, despite his engaging manner, there lurks beneath his skin a sometimes tense and pessimistic nature. The Goat can be a worrier and without the support and encouragement of others can feel insecure and be hesitant in his actions.

To make the most of himself and his abilities the Goat should aim to become more assertive and decisive as well as more at ease with himself. He has much in his favour but he really does need to promote himself more and aim to be bolder in his actions. He would also be helped if he were to sort out his priorities and set about his activities in an organized and disciplined manner. There are some Goats who tend to be haphazard in the way they go about things and this can hamper their progress.

Although the Goat will always value the support and backing of others, it would also be in his interests to become more independent in his actions and not be so reticent about striking out on his own. He does, after all, possess many talents as well as a sincere and likeable personality and by always giving of his best, he can make his life rich, rewarding and enjoyable.

Advice for the Goat's Year Ahead

GENERAL PROSPECTS

A tricky year ahead. This is a year in which the Goat needs to proceed with care and avoid undue risks. Any progress he makes will come from careful and applied effort.

CAREER PROSPECTS

In 1997 progress is possible but may not always be easy. However, some of the events that happen will help the Goat to consider his present position and the direction he is heading in, and will give him a new incentive and greater resolve to make the most of himself and his abilities. With determination and a willingness to adapt to changing situations, he will, as the year progresses, acquit himself well and sow the seeds for future advancement.

FINANCE

Considerable care is needed. This is just not a year in which the Goat can take risks with his money and should he have any doubts over any financial matter he should check the details carefully. It would also be in his interests to keep a close watch over his level of spending.

RELATIONS WITH OTHERS

In 1997 the Goat will obtain much useful advice and encouragement from his family and friends and, if he does have any problems or uncertainties, he should not hesitate to seek their opinions. Domestically and socially, this will be a generally busy, sometimes fraught year, but in spite of this the Goat can look forward to some enjoyable and meaningful times with those around him. The main thing in 1997 is that he should not bottle up his own feelings and concerns but be open and forthcoming with others. Goats seeking friends should make every effort to go out more and perhaps join a local society or club. Effort on their part will lead to some enjoyable occasions and new and sometimes important friendships.

THE MONKEY

Lively, enterprising and innovative, the Monkey certainly knows how to impress. He has wide interests, a good sense of fun and relates well to others. He also possesses a shrewd mind and often has a happy knack of turning events and situations to his advantage.

However, despite his versatility and considerable gifts, the Monkey does have his weaknesses. He often lacks persistence, can get distracted easily and also places tremendous reliance upon his own judgement. While his belief in himself is a commendable asset, it would certainly be in the Monkey's interests to be more mindful of the advice and views of others. Also, while he likes to keep tabs on all that is going on around him, he can be evasive and secretive with regard to his own feelings and activities, and again a more forthcoming attitude would be to his advantage.

The Monkey also possesses a most enterprising nature, although in his desire to succeed he can sometimes be tempted to cut corners or be crafty. He should recognize that such actions can rebound on him!

However, the Monkey is resourceful and his sheer

strength of character will lead him to an interesting and varied life. If he can channel his considerable energies wisely and overcome his sometimes restless tendencies, his life can be crowned with success and achievement. Added to which, with his amiable personality, he will enjoy the friendship of many.

Advice for the Monkey's Year Ahead

GENERAL PROSPECTS

An interesting year ahead. Although the Monkey's progress may not always be as great as he would like, he will gain much of value over the year and usefully extend his experience. Also, much of what he learns in the Ox year will help to prepare the way for the more considerable advances he will make in the next few years.

CAREER PROSPECTS

The Ox year rewards the hard-working and if the Monkey is prepared to give of his best and set about his activities in his usual enterprising manner, then he can make progress. However, throughout the year, he needs to be organized and prepared to adapt to new situations as they arise. As a resourceful Monkey, he will find new situations lead to new opportunities! However, while he can improve his position over the year, his greatest gains will come from the experience he obtains. It is an excellent year for him to add to his skills and qualifications.

FINANCE

In 1997 the Monkey would do well to monitor his level of

spending and avoid getting involved in risky or speculative undertakings. Generally, he will fare reasonably well in financial matters but care and a certain restraint are most definitely needed.

RELATIONS WITH OTHERS

Domestically, this will be a busy year for the Monkey and while his family will give him much valuable encouragement, he would do well to listen closely to their views and advice. Although the Monkey may like to do things his own way, he will gain much from the input of others. Also, without due consideration of the interests of others, differences could well arise – Monkeys, take note! The Monkey's social life will generally go well, with some opportunities for new friendships, but again, to preserve good relations, he must pay close attention to the views and feelings of others.

THE ROOSTER

With his considerable bearing and incisive and resolute manner, the Rooster makes an impressive figure. He has a sharp mind, keeps well-informed on many matters and expresses himself clearly and convincingly. He is meticulous and efficient in his undertakings and commands much respect. He also has a genuine and caring interest in others.

The Rooster has much in his favour but there are some aspects of his character that can tell against him. He can be candid in his views and sometimes over-zealous in his actions, and without forethought he can say or do things he later regrets. His high standards also make him fussy – even pedantic – and he can get diverted onto relatively minor matters when, in truth, he could be occupying his time more profitably. This is something all Roosters would do well to watch. Also, while the Rooster is a great planner, he can sometimes be unrealistic in his expectations. In making plans – indeed, with most of his activities – the Rooster would do well to consult with others rather than keep his thoughts to himself. By doing so, he will greatly benefit from their input.

The Rooster has considerable talents as well as a commendable drive and commitment, but to make the most of himself he does need to channel his energies wisely and watch his candid and sometimes volatile nature. With care, he can make a success of his life, and with his wide interests and outgoing personality will enjoy the friendship and respect of many.

Advice for the Rooster's Year Ahead

GENERAL PROSPECTS
The Rooster can look forward to a distinct upturn in his fortunes this year and he should pursue his aims and objectives with a resolute determination. The aspects are most encouraging and he should do all he can to take advantage of the positive trends that prevail. For those Roosters who may not have fared so well in recent years, this means putting past reversals behind them and setting about their activities with new vigour and optimism. The Rooster possesses many talents and in 1997 he should make sure he uses them well.

CAREER PROSPECTS

The determined and enterprising Rooster can accomplish much over the year. Throughout 1997 he should promote himself, his plans and ideas as much as he can – those around him think highly of him and this will be a year when both his past and present efforts will be recognized and rewarded. It is a year of progress and the Rooster should give of his best and actively pursue the opportunities that the year will bring.

FINANCE

A good year for financial matters. If the Rooster has any spare money at his disposal, he would do well to consider putting it towards a specific purpose such as travel or home improvements, or saving it for his long-term future. However, while his finances will show an improvement, if he enters into a large agreement he still needs to check the details carefully. Bureaucratic matters – and this can involve finance – could, without care, prove problematical.

RELATIONS WITH OTHERS

This will be a pleasing year for domestic matters and the Rooster will be considerably heartened by the support and encouragement given by those around him. In return, he should take note of any advice he receives, particularly from those senior to him. They do so want him to succeed and make the most of himself and he should consider their words well. A promising year, too, for social matters and over the year the Rooster can look forward to attending several enjoyable parties and functions. For the young and unattached Rooster, the aspects for making friends and romance are good.

THE DOG

Loyal, dependable and with a good understanding of human nature, the Dog is well placed to win the respect and admiration of many. He is a no nonsense sort of person and hates any sort of hypocrisy and falsehood. With the Dog you know where you stand and, given his direct manner, where he stands on any issue. He also has a strong humanitarian nature and often champions good and just causes.

The Dog has many fine attributes, although there are certain traits that can prevent him from either enjoying or making the most of his life. He is a great worrier and can get anxious over all manner of things. Although it may not always be easy, the Dog should try to rid himself of the 'worry habit'. When tense or concerned, he should be more prepared to speak to others rather than shoulder his worries all by himself. In some cases, they could even be of his own making! Also, the Dog has a tendency to look on the pessimistic side of things and he would certainly be helped if he were to look more optimistically on his undertakings. He does, after all, possess many skills and should justifiably have faith in his abilities. Another weakness is his tendency to be stubborn over certain issues. If he is not careful, this stubbornness could at times undermine his position.

If the Dog can reduce the worrying and pessimistic side

of his nature, then he will not only enjoy life more but find he is achieving more as a result. He possesses a truly admirable character and his loyalty, reliability and sincerity are appreciated by all he meets. In his life he will do much good and befriend many – and he owes it to himself to enjoy life too. Sometimes it might help him to recall the words of another Dog, Winston Churchill: 'When I look back on all these worries I remember the story of the old man who said on his deathbed that he had had a lot of trouble in his life, most of which never happened.'

Advice for the Dog's Year Ahead

GENERAL PROSPECTS

In 1997 the Dog will need to proceed carefully and cautiously. This is not a year for taking undue risks. However, events will enable him to reflect upon his present situation and give some thought to his future aspirations. Some of the things that the Dog decides in 1997, as well as achieves, will be of considerable help to his future progress. This may not be the easiest of years but it can be a constructive one.

CAREER PROSPECTS

This will be a year of modest progress. However, throughout the year the Dog must act in close co-operation with others and be prepared to adapt to changing situations. This is not a year in which he can take risks or be too independent or inflexible in his actions. His greatest gains will come through the experience he obtains and any additional skills he is able to acquire. What he learns in

1997 will do much to further his prospects as the more favourable Tiger year approaches. This is also a good year for the Dog to think and plan out his future – some of the ideas he has could prove of great value in the years ahead.

FINANCE
Considerable care is needed. This is not a year for taking risks, getting involved in speculative matters or for lending to others. In 1997 the Dog must keep close watch over his level of spending and when facing large expenses, particularly concerning his accommodation and transport, it would be in his interests to obtain prices and quotations from several different sources.

RELATIONS WITH OTHERS
Throughout the year the Dog must remain mindful of the views and interests of others and listen closely to any advice he is given. Those around him do think highly of him and speak with his best interests at heart. Domestically and socially, this can be a gratifying year for him and his family life will give rise to some pleasurable and memorable occasions. However, if a difference should arise he should aim to resolve this quickly and amicably rather than allow it to linger in the background. Similarly, to preserve good relations, he should avoid being too stubborn or intransigent over relatively minor issues or when facing change. With care, his relations with others can generally go well and provide him with much pleasure.

THE PIG

Genial, sincere and trusting, the Pig gets on well with most. He has a kind and caring nature, a dislike of discord and often possesses a good sense of humour. In addition, he has a fondness for socializing and enjoying the good life!

The Pig also possesses a shrewd mind, is particularly adept in dealing with business and financial matters, and has a robust and resilient nature. Although not all his plans in life may work out as he would like, he is tenacious and will often rise up and succeed after experiencing setbacks and difficulties. In his often active and varied life he can accomplish much, although there are certain aspects of his character that can tell against him. If he can modify or keep these areas in check then his life will certainly be easier and possibly even more successful.

In his activities the Pig can sometimes overcommit himself and while he does not want to disappoint, he would certainly be helped if he were to set about his activities in an organized and systematic manner and give himself priorities at busy times. He should also not allow others to take advantage of his good nature and it would be in his interests if he were sometimes more discerning. There will have been times when he has been gullible and naïve; fortunately, though, the Pig quickly learns from his mistakes. He also possesses a stubborn streak and if new situations do not fit in with his line of thinking, he can be inflexible. Such an attitude may not always be to his advantage.

The Pig is a great pleasure-seeker and while he should deservedly enjoy the fruits of his labours, he can sometimes be indulgent and extravagant. This is again some-thing he would do well to watch.

However, though the Pig may possess some faults, those who come into contact with him are invariably impressed by his integrity, amiable manner and intelligence. If he uses his talents wisely, his life can be crowned with con-siderable achievement and the good-hearted Pig will also be loved and respected by many.

Advice for the Pig's Year Ahead

GENERAL PROSPECTS

This is a year when the Pig should actively set about pursuing his goals and aspirations. Great things can be achieved in the Ox year and the Pig should make the most of the progressive trends that prevail. Personally, too, the year will contain some pleasing times.

CAREER PROSPECTS

In 1997 the Pig should put his skills and past experience to good use and aim to improve upon his present position. Determined action on his part will produce positive results. Similarly, those Pigs seeking work should stay alert for openings to pursue and, if need be, approach those who can help and advise. By using his initiative and actively promoting himself the Pig can gain much over the year.

FINANCE

A good year for financial matters. While the Pig will undoubtedly enjoy this improvement, he would do well to consider setting some money aside for specific purposes and also saving for his longer term future. The savings he makes now could build into a useful asset in years to come.

RELATIONS WITH OTHERS

Personally, 1997 will be a year of much happiness for the Pig. Both his domestic and social life will go well and those close to him will give him much useful advice and encouragement. There will also be romantic opportunities for those Pigs who are unattached. The summer months in particular will be an especially favourable time for all Pigs.